Winning
Tennis

The Smarter Player's Guide

Winning Tennis

The Smarter Player's Guide

Rob Antoun

APPLE

First published in the UK in 2013 by
Apple Press Ltd
7 Greenland Street
London NW1 0ND
www.apple-press.com

A Marshall Edition
Conceived, edited, and designed by
Marshall Editions
The Old Brewery
6 Blundell Street
London N7 9BH
www.marshalleditions.com

ISBN: 978-1-84543-470-0

Current printing (last digit)
10 9 8 7 6 5 4 3 2 1

For Marshall Editions
Publisher James Ashton-Tyler
Editorial Director Sorrel Wood
Project Editor Caroline West, Bluedragonfly Ltd.
Design and Cover Design Mark Latter, Bluedragonfly Ltd.
Photography Simon Pask
Editorial Assistant Philippa Davis
Production Manager Nikki Ingram

Originated in Hong Kong by Modern Age.
Printed and bound in China by 1010 Printing International Ltd.

Cover image: Antenna/Getty Images

CONTENTS

INTRODUCTION

When we decide to improve our game in tennis, we usually spend extra time practising how to hit the ball with more speed, accuracy and consistency. But tennis is both a sending and receiving sport, which means that 50 per cent of your time is spent preparing for the ball to be hit towards you. The most successful players are the ones who use these split seconds of preparation time most effectively – they are the best receivers of the ball. If you become a better receiver, you will be more able to anticipate what shot your opponent will hit, perceive the oncoming ball quickly and clearly, and then prepare your return in the best possible position on the court. During the course of a match your opponent will give you numerous visual clues as to how and where they are most likely to hit the ball. This book will help you to read these clues, allowing you to hit a better return – and win more games with the skills you already have.

This book is unique, because it doesn't tell you how to hit a tennis ball. Specifically aimed at competitive weekend players, it focuses purely on what your opponent is doing, allowing you to maximize your success in any game quickly and easily. It highlights the shots your opponent will mostly likely hit from a variety of game situations and examines them with expert technical and tactical analysis. *Winning Tennis* will show you how to anticipate a shot based on your opponent's court position, grip and swing, as well as how to pick up clues to his or her favourite playing patterns. You will also learn how the flight of the oncoming ball should influence your preparation and court positioning, and be guided as to what shot you might hit back based on what you see coming towards you.

Divided into the five main playing situations in tennis, this book gives advice on improving your game play while serving, returning, playing at the baseline, approaching and playing at the net and what to do when your opponent approaches the net. Each section will look at the potential shots you can hit based on what your opponent is planning to do – with numerous photos and diagrams to help explain each scenario.

At the front of the book you will learn the basic techniques for how to read the game, using anticipation and perception skills that will help you scrutinize your opponent's movements and the oncoming ball even more closely. It will also recommend how to improve and develop your decision-making skills – including a system that helps you build a portfolio of tactical responses to any playing situation.

The final chapter focuses on common game styles in tennis and highlights the key methods of play used by the world's best players – and how you can apply these methods to your game. Here you will find specific ways to play against each particular game style so you will always be able to find a solution against the trickiest of opponents.

I hope you enjoy winning more games of tennis!

Rob Antoun

➲ **Reading the game**
Novak Djokovic is a master at both receiving and sending the ball.

HOW TO USE
THIS BOOK

You don't need to read this book from front to back – go straight to the section that interests you most. Think about the different types of play – serving, returning, playing from the baseline and at the net – and where your strengths and weaknesses lie. Consider what part of the court you are the most comfortable playing from and which tactical situation you need the most help with.

Key things to consider These panels highlight each section's key points with helpful reminders on what you can do to improve your game.

What to look for Easy-to-spot panels highlight photographs that show you what your opponent is doing.

Annotated photographs 'Highlighter' marks draw attention to the key things to look for.

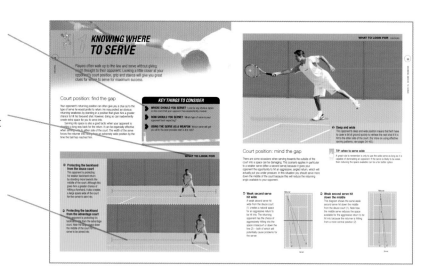

Singles or doubles? Most of the advice in this book can be followed whether you are playing singles or doubles. Clear headings indicate whether the advice given is more suitable for singles or doubles play.

Patterns of play Written for either singles or doubles games, these are ready-to-use game plans you can use to win in specific situations.

Tip and practice panels Each chapter has tips on improving your skills and suggests practice games you can play in training to get the most from the techniques in the book.

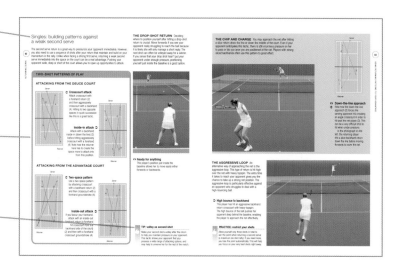

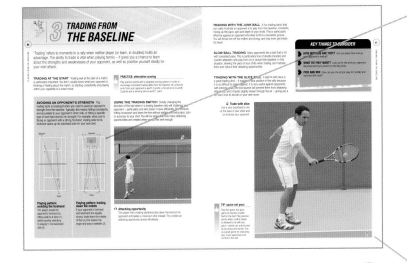

Court diagrams In every case, 'player' represents 'you' and appears at the bottom of the diagram, while your 'opponent' always appears at the top of the diagram. In the Serving and Returning Serve chapters – you, the 'player', changes to 'server' or 'returner'.

Player icon The circle in the corner of some photos indicates pictures that demonstrate advice for you, the player, rather than showing your opponent.

KEY TO COURT DIAGRAMS

Throughout the book, court diagrams illustrate typical playing scenarios, shot sequences and patterns of play. The symbols used are the same throughout the book.

○ Player's starting position	○ Opponent's starting position
X Player's doubles partner	X Opponent's doubles partner
→ Player's shot	→ Opponent's shot
⇢ Player's movement	⇢ Opponent's movement
Numbers indicate the sequence of play	Target area

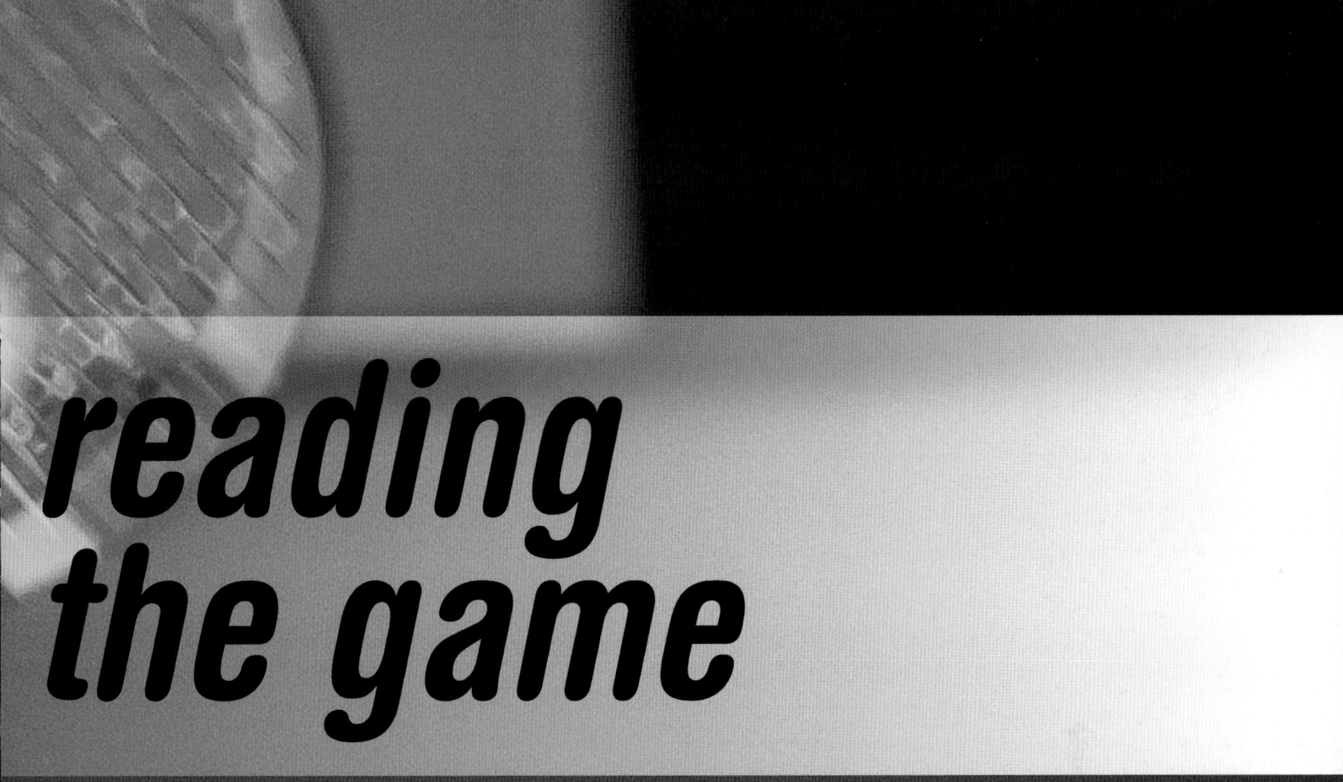

reading the game

The ability to 'read the game' is a valuable skill that is often talked about but very rarely taught. It may surprise you how easily paying more attention to every ball you send and receive can be turned into a real weapon and greatly improve your chances of winning. This chapter looks at the key skills that can help you to play more successfully, as well as what 'reading the game' really means.

1 What does reading the game really mean?

The game of tennis is as much about receiving the ball as it is about sending it. This section teaches you how to prepare best for the oncoming ball, both physically and mentally, which means getting into the best ready position and condition possible before hitting every shot.

See pages 12–13

2 Anticipation and perception

Being able to predict what shot your opponent is about to hit will give you a massive advantage in any rally. This section looks at the different types of anticipation you can use against a variety of opponents, as well as how to prepare for your next shot by quickly perceiving the characteristics of the oncoming ball.

See pages 14–17

3 Smart decision-making

Once you have used your anticipation and perception skills to good effect, then it is time to decide which shot you are going to hit! This invaluable section explains a simple method by which you can establish exactly what shot to use depending on the type of situation you are in.

See pages 18–19

1 WHAT DOES READING THE GAME REALLY MEAN?

A player who can read the game of tennis holds a massive advantage over an opponent. Reading the game means being able to anticipate what is most likely to happen on the next shot, in the next game and over the course of a match – allowing you to react swiftly and efficiently, and to make smart decisions as a result.

As a player who can read the game, you will understand how each of your shots will affect your opponent and how he is likely to react, allowing you to use specific, repeatable tactics and strategies to great effect. It also means being aware of how the different game styles in tennis match up – helping you maximize your strengths and limit the exposure of your weaknesses as a result.

The ability to plan ahead often helps you remain in control of your emotions because you have a better sense of what might happen next. Reducing fear of the unknown goes a long way towards helping you build feelings of confidence and commitment – no matter what the scoreboard says.

Reading the game also means reading your opponent's emotions. Looking out for the subtle physical and psychological messages that your opponent sends out during a match will raise your awareness of how he is thinking and feeling. Anger, frustration or fear, for example, are exhibited in a number of different ways, and knowing exactly how your opponent feels will directly affect whether you choose to attack, defend or trade with him next.

Ultimately, reading the game well puts you one shot ahead of your opponent. The following pages look at how you can achieve this by developing your receiving skills – which require good anticipation and perception, as well as excellent decision-making abilities.

KEY THINGS TO CONSIDER

▶ **KNOW YOUR GAME** Try to understand your own strengths and weaknesses as this will help you make the best shot selection every time.

▶ **MORE KNOWLEDGE, LESS FEAR** The more you can learn about your opponent (before and/ or during the match), the less fearful you will be about how he might play against you.

↻ **Good anticipation skills**
Looking carefully at how your opponent is shaping up to hit the ball will give you a massive advantage every time you play. This player is anticipating what his opponent is about to do next and is preparing to receive the ball.

Developing receiving skills

In tennis, it is easy to forget that a player only hits the ball 50 per cent of the time. The remaining 50 per cent of the rally is spent receiving the ball. It's interesting how the vast majority of coaching resources dedicated to helping players improve their games focus purely on the sending skills of the sport.

WORKING WITH A COACH Coaches are at their best giving technical instructions on how to hit the ball. This is because the sending of the ball is very visual. Grips, swings and stances can all be analyzed in great detail and improvements can be seen and felt straight away. However, improving a player's receiving skills is trickier. This is because much of the process of receiving a ball starts in a player's head, so it is much harder to monitor progress. As a result, this crucial part of the game is often overlooked.

YOUR READY POSITION From a physical standpoint, to receive the ball well you need to start by using a good ready position. This means keeping your knees flexed (try to keep your knees feeling soft) with your feet around shoulder-width apart. Lower your head (around one head height lower than normal) and keep it still and slightly in front of your body.

As your opponent is about to hit the ball, you'll also want to use a well-timed split-step. This is a very subtle jump that you make to centre your body weight so that you are balanced and ready to move in any direction for the ball. The jump effectively shifts your centre of gravity higher so that you can move quickly and nimbly. Ideally, you want to regain this ready position and use a split-step each time your opponent is about to hit the ball – no matter where you are positioned on the court.

○ **Working with a coach**
Ask your coach to help you with your receiving skills as well as your sending skills.

○ **A good ready position**
Try to create a balanced physical platform from which to move.

⊃ **A good ready condition**
Always maintain a sharp focus every time you are about to hit the ball.

YOUR READY CONDITION Your mental condition is just as important as your physical position. Maintain a sharp focus on your opponent before he hits the ball (anticipation, see pages 14–15) and then track the ball as soon as it leaves his racket strings (perception, see pages 16–17). Focusing your mind on these two things will allow you to make the best shot selection every time (decision-making, see pages 18–19).

2 ANTICIPATION AND PERCEPTION

During the split-second process of information gathering, use your anticipation skills – both tactical and technical – as a powerful mental weapon to help you assess your opponent's most likely shot. You can then use your skills of perception to track your opponent's actual shot. Using this combination of skills effectively will give you more time to prepare for and execute your shot.

Using tactical anticipation

Your tactical anticipation is based on the court position that your opponent is taking, the previous ball you hit (if there was one) and the previous playing patterns of your opponent.

TRACK YOUR OPPONENT'S COURT POSITION Where your opponent is standing on the court will give you a big clue to what he intends to do with his next shot. For example, if he is playing from well inside the baseline, there is every chance he will want to attack from there. If he is very deep behind the baseline, then he will have a far smaller chance of attacking, even if he wants to.

WHAT SHOT IS COMING NEXT? As you become more experienced you will start to develop a sense of what to expect next from your opponent based on your last shot. For example, if you hit the ball short by mistake, you will automatically start to anticipate a more aggressive play from your opponent. If you have been the aggressor you may naturally sense a weaker next shot from your opponent.

REMEMBER PREVIOUS PLAYING PATTERNS Experienced tennis players will use their opponent's previous playing patterns (both in the current match and/or in previous ones) as a way of anticipating their next shot. For example, if an opponent has only hit his passing shots crosscourt each time you have approached the net, you would be smart to make sure you can cover the crosscourt pass next time you approach.

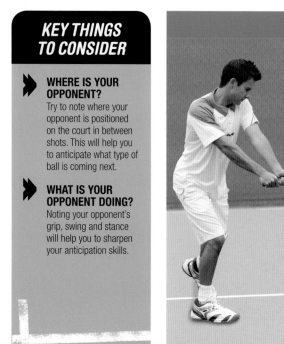

KEY THINGS TO CONSIDER

▶ **WHERE IS YOUR OPPONENT?**
Try to note where your opponent is positioned on the court in between shots. This will help you to anticipate what type of ball is coming next.

▶ **WHAT IS YOUR OPPONENT DOING?**
Noting your opponent's grip, swing and stance will help you to sharpen your anticipation skills.

WHAT TO LOOK FOR

☊ **An opponent under pressure**
An open racket face indicates that your opponent is under significant pressure on the baseline.

☋ **An opponent planning to attack**
If your opponent steps forwards into the court, then he will often be looking to attack with his next shot.

Using technical anticipation

Technical anticipation also occurs the moment before your opponent hits the ball and aims to identify the technique that he is looking to use. As you develop your receiving skills you will start to anticipate your opponent's next shot simply by observing how he is holding his racket, making his swing or using a particular stance.

SPOT THE GRIP The grip your opponent uses will have a massive effect on what he can and can't do with the ball. For example, an opponent who uses a forehand grip to serve with will always struggle to create enough spin on the second serve. This means that he will need to take a lot of pace off the shot in order to hit the ball in safely. You can anticipate a slower serve as a result.

LOOK FOR THE SWING The swing that your opponent prepares with will also give you a big clue as to what is coming next. For example, an opponent who uses a big backswing on the forehand side is looking to create power more than anything else. If this is done at the right time, you can anticipate an aggressive shot coming at you.

CHECK OUT THE STANCE Although perhaps harder to see, your opponent's stance (the way his feet are positioned) will also give you a potential clue as to the type of shot he is looking to hit. For example, if he uses a closed stance on his forehand (his front foot is positioned across his back foot), it is far less likely that he will be able to hit an effective crosscourt ball. This is because his hips are prevented from rotating enough to create the crosscourt angle on the ball.

These points are all looked at in more detail in later chapters.

WHAT TO LOOK FOR

↻ Your opponent's swing
The size of your opponent's swing can indicate how hard she is going to hit the ball.

↻ Your opponent's stance
How your opponent sets up to hit will often indicate the likely direction of her shot. In this case, the opponent is most likely to hit a defensive shot since she has been put under a lot of pressure.

↻ Your opponent's grip
The grip that your opponent is using will strongly influence the type of spin she can put on the ball.

PRACTICE: better anticipation skills
Allow one point per game to be won through good anticipation. At any time during a rally call out where you think your practice partner will hit his next shot. If you are right, you win the point automatically. Do this by shouting "stop" before your partner hits the ball and then tell him what you think he was about to do. This drill is really useful for both players.

Sharpening your perception

You need to perceive the characteristics of the oncoming ball the moment it leaves your opponent's racket strings. Often, less experienced players won't really start to recognize the ball's characteristics before it crosses the net and starts to bounce in front of them. By this time it is too late, and this will put pressure on your shot-making ability and on the decisions you make.

Remember that there are two ball flights to track when you are playing from the baseline – one from your opponent's racket to the bounce and one from the bounce to your racket. Both of these ball flights will give you vital clues as to how you should prepare for your next shot. To fully understand how to perceive the ball, start by looking at the five possible ball characteristics in tennis.

HEIGHT This is one of the first things you will perceive about the ball as it is hit by your opponent and should give you a good indication as to whether you can attack the oncoming ball or need to defend against it. Use the net as a natural reference point to help you judge the ball's height each time.

DIRECTION The path of the ball will indicate whether you should prepare to hit a forehand or a backhand (either a groundstroke or a volley, depending on your court position). Spotting the ball's direction as quickly as possible will help you prepare more effectively.

DEPTH How far the oncoming ball will travel can be difficult to judge and is often the characteristic that is perceived at the last moment of the ball's flight. The ability to prepare by moving out of a space (against a deep ball) and moving into a space (against a short ball) is important and is often the key ingredient in helping you prepare well for your next shot.

SPEED How fast the ball is travelling determines how much time you will have to prepare for your next shot. The key thing to remember here is that your preparation should mirror the speed of the oncoming ball. For example, use a quick and simple backswing on your return when you face a fast first serve or a longer and smoother backswing against an opponent's slower and higher-bouncing groundstroke.

SPIN More experienced players will hit with different types of spin (on groundstrokes and serves in particular) and these will create a different movement on the ball as a result. A ball hit with topspin will kick higher than normal after bouncing, whereas a ball hit with slice will stay lower and slide across the court after bouncing. You may be able to anticipate the type of spin that is coming based on the technique that your opponent is using to hit the ball with (technical anticipation, see page 15).

⌒ Which direction?
Reading the ball's direction as soon as it leaves your opponent's racket will help you prepare for either a forehand or backhand. This opponent is hitting crosscourt to a right-hander's backhand side.

⌒ How deep?
Depth can be a tricky characteristic to read, so study the ball's trajectory as soon as it is hit by your opponent to see how deep it may bounce. This opponent has been caught off guard by how deep the ball has bounced.

⌒ How fast?
Increasing the speed of the ball will reduce the amount of time your opponent has to prepare. Hitting a smash is one of the best ways to hit with speed.

PRACTICE: perceiving ball characteristics

This drill will help you sharpen your perception skills and make you more aware of the different ball characteristics as the ball is hit towards you. With a practice partner, take it in turns to call out a specific ball characteristic as soon as you see it. For example, if perceiving height, call "high", "medium" or "low" before the ball crosses your side of the net. If perceiving direction, call "left" or "right" and if perceiving depth, call "short", "middle" or "deep" as soon as you can. This will help you focus on the oncoming ball and receive it effectively. Playing other ball sports such as soccer, basketball and hockey may also help because they require many similar anticipation and perception skills.

How high?
The height of the ball is probably the first characteristic you will spot as it is hit by your opponent. Once you spot a ball with a high flight path you can move forwards to volley it out of the air.

What type of spin?
Carefully watch your opponent's racket preparation to gain an insight into the type of spin that may be used on the ball.

3 SMART DECISION-MAKING

Use a combination of great anticipation and perception skills to make smart decisions every time you hit the ball. This is a crucial skill that separates the best from the rest. Having an objective tactical conversation in your head allows you to stay calm and focused, and so concentrate on every point. It will also help prevent emotions such as nervousness, frustration or anxiety from taking over.

Player tracks opponent's shot
Where and how you hit your next ball will be strongly influenced by your opponent's previous shot.

Player returns opponent's shot
How you position yourself on the court will depend very much on the shot you have just hit.

PRACTICE: action replay

To help guide your decision-making, try keeping a spare ball in your pocket when you play practice points. If you make an error, take out the spare ball and position yourself where you made the error from on the court. Now you have to decide – was it a poor decision that caused the error or just a poor shot? If it was a poor decision, re-start the point by choosing to play a different shot; if it was a poor shot but a good decision, then re-start the point by playing the same shot again.

ESTABLISHING A RULE You will base your decision on how and where to hit your next shot on four key factors: your previous shot (if there was one), your opponent's previous shot, your court position and your opponent's court position. Individual players will develop their own set of rules based around these four factors, which will influence the types of decisions they make.

Creating a tactical rule enables you to start playing with more confidence and security, as well as to define more specific patterns of play around your own strengths and weaknesses as you become more experienced.

For example: a player might create the rule of 'defending deep crosscourt with slice when under pressure on my backhand side at the baseline'. Creating this rule allows him to focus more on his shot-making skill as soon as he is in this position in a rally, because he has already made the decision. After hitting this shot he will get feedback about how successful it was and will decide to either use the same tactic again or change it next time he is in the same position. So, the rule is constantly being evaluated and fine-tuned as the player gains more experience of the game.

◑ Player's court position: preparing to attack
If you sense your previous shot has been effective, you may want to take up a more aggressive court position.

... AND AN 'EXCEPT IF' RULE As a tactical rule becomes more established and used more frequently, there will also be exceptions that will change a player's decision. In the previous example, if the player spots his opponent approaching the net, he may change his decision and choose to hit with topspin down the middle of the court instead. So, the same rule applies, but an 'except if' clause has also been created. Experienced players will continue to build a series of rules and 'except ifs' that allow them to make good decisions based around their own specific game style. If you do this you will have a solution – or at least an attempt at a solution – for almost every potential playing situation in the game.

WHAT TO LOOK FOR

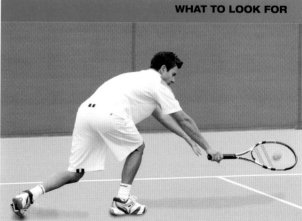

◑ Opponent's court position: on the defensive
Reading your opponent's court position will help you to prepare well for your next shot. This opponent is struggling to return a ball that has been hit wide and low.

serving

The serve is unique because it is the one shot that you have total control over. As the serving player, you have the chance to think carefully about how and where to hit the ball, which will give you a great opportunity to gain the upper hand over your opponent right away. It is crucial to use this precious thinking time as effectively as possible. This chapter looks at the three keys to successful serving.

1 Knowing where to serve

Look closely at where and how your opponent is standing to work out the type of serve he would prefer to receive, as well as the type of return he'd prefer to hit. Key things to look out for are your opponent's court position, grip and stance.

See pages 22–31

2 Using variety as a weapon

The most effective servers aren't always the ones who hit the ball the hardest. You can often win service games simply by keeping your opponent guessing. This section looks at the consequences of changing the direction, pace and spin of your serve.

See pages 32–33

3 Using serving patterns

Try to view your serve as the first shot in a winning pattern of play rather than just a way to start the next point. This section looks at how you can combine your serve with other shots to create successful, repeatable patterns of play.

See pages 34–45

KNOWING WHERE
TO SERVE

Players often walk up to the line and serve without giving much thought to their opponent. Looking a little closer at your opponent's court position, grip and stance will give you great clues for where to serve for maximum success.

Court position: find the gap

Your opponent's returning position can often give you a clue as to the type of serve he would prefer to return. He may protect an obvious returning weakness by standing in a position that gives him a greater chance to hit his favoured shot. However, doing so can inadvertently create extra space for you to serve into.

Serving into space is also a good tactic when your opponent is standing a long way back for the return. It can be especially effective when serving wide to either side of the court. The width of the serve forces the returner into hitting from an extremely wide position by the time the ball has reached him.

KEY THINGS TO CONSIDER

 WHERE SHOULD YOU SERVE? Look for any obvious space on the court that your opponent has inadvertently created.

 HOW SHOULD YOU SERVE? Which type of serve is your opponent least expecting?

USING THE SERVE AS A WEAPON Which serve will get you off to the best possible start in the rally?

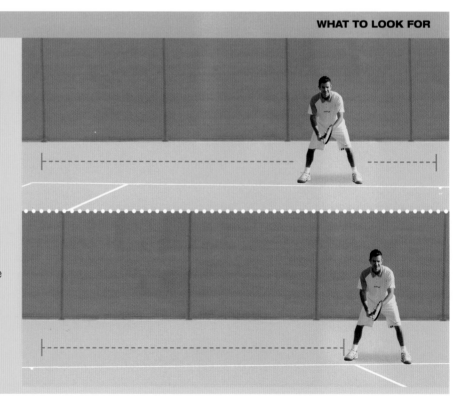

WHAT TO LOOK FOR

➲ **Protecting the backhand from the deuce court**
This opponent is protecting his weaker backhand return by standing more towards the middle of the court. Although this gives him a greater chance of hitting a forehand, it also creates a large space wide of the court for the server to aim into.

➲ **Protecting the backhand from the advantage court**
This opponent is protecting his backhand side from the advantage court. Note the large space down the middle of the court for the serve to be aimed into.

Deep and wide
This opponent's deep and wide position means that he'll have to cover a lot of ground quickly to retrieve the next shot if it is hit to the other side of the court. (For more on using effective serving patterns, see pages 34–45.)

Court position: mind the gap

There are some occasions when serving towards the outside of the court into a space can be damaging. This scenario applies in particular to a weaker serve (often a second serve) because it gives your opponent the opportunity to hit an aggressive, angled return, which will actually put you under pressure. In this situation you should serve more down the middle of the court because this will reduce the returning angle available to your opponent.

TIP: when to serve wide
A great rule to remember is only to use the wide serve as long as it is capable of dominating an opponent. If the serve is likely to be weak, then reducing the space available can be a far better option.

Weak second serve hit wide
A weak second serve hit wide from the deuce court (1) creates a natural space for an aggressive return to be hit into. The returning opponent has the choice of aggressively hitting into the space crosscourt or down the line (2) – both of which will potentially cause problems for the server.

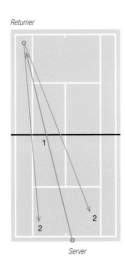
Returner
Server

Weak second serve hit down the middle
This diagram shows the same weak second serve hit down the middle from the deuce court (1). Note how the middle serve reduces the space available for the aggressive return to be hit into because the returner is hitting from a more central position (2).

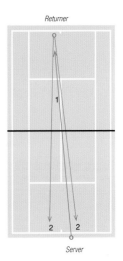
Returner
Server

Court position: close the gap

There will be times when serving straight at your opponent is an option, although your serve must be strong enough to prevent him making space for his own shot. This type of approach is often effective against tall players who like to make contact with the ball further away from their body or players who stand well inside the baseline to return serve.

It can also be very effective against opponents who hit with a single-handed backhand. This type of opponent prefers to make contact with the ball further in front of and away from his body, compared with the double-hander who can afford to make contact with the ball closer to his body.

POSITIONING THE BALL	WHAT TO LOOK FOR

↻ **Close to the body**
The ball is hit close to the body, preventing the opponent from hitting fully through the ball. This will often result in a shorter, more defensive return being played.

↻ **Too much space**
Note the space here between the ball and the body of the opponent with this contact point, which allows him to swing freely through the ball.

↻ **Single-handed backhand return**
The ball is hit close to the body, meaning the racket often gets swung across the ball rather than straight through it. This type of return is likely to drift down the line rather than crosscourt from the advantage court and drift across the court more from the deuce side. A more experienced opponent may be forced into abbreviating his swing.

↻ **Double-handed backhand return**
Because the swing path of the double-hander is shorter this opponent can afford to hit the ball closer to his body without compromising the shot, and can generate more power and control. This is one of the key reasons why the double-handed backhand has become such a weapon in today's game.

Your opponent's grip: when returning serve

The grip that your opponent uses to return serve will impact greatly on the type of return that he hits back. It also gives you a clue about the type of return that he wants to hit. The panel below looks at the grips an opponent might use to return serve, with the top photographs showing what the returner will look like from a player's perspective.

For more advice on exploiting your opponent's grip: see pages 28–29 (when serving against double-handed grips); pages 70–73 (when you are attacking from the baseline); and pages 80–81 (when you are defending from the baseline).

YOUR OPPONENT'S RETURNING GRIP

WHAT TO LOOK FOR

○ Eastern forehand returner
This opponent will struggle to produce power and spin with this grip when the ball bounces at shoulder height.

○ Semi-western forehand returner
Opponents should be tested low, wide and high to find out their weakest position when using this grip.

○ Western forehand returner
An opponent using this forehand grip may struggle to deal with balls that bounce low and wide.

○ Eastern forehand grip
Players who favour their forehand often use this common forehand grip to return with. Your opponent will find this grip effective on wide and low balls, as well as short balls where he can move through the shot. However, he will find it more difficult to produce power and spin when the ball bounces up to shoulder height.

○ Semi-western forehand grip
Many experienced players use this versatile grip on their forehand side. It can be adapted to suit a variety of contact points and also enables your opponent to generate pace and spin on the ball. This grip may make it more difficult for your opponent to hit balls above shoulder height, although you should test him low, wide and high to find his weakest position.

○ Western forehand grip
An extreme version of the semi-western grip, with the back of the hand placed underneath the grip. Used by experienced players on high-bouncing courts like clay, it is particularly effective on high-bouncing balls, as well as for generating lots of spin. However, your opponent may find it difficult to deal with balls that bounce low and wide if he is using this grip.

⌓ 50:50 backhand returner
Serving wide may prevent opponents using the 50:50 grip reaching the ball in time.

⌓ Eastern backhand returner
An opponent using this grip may struggle with higher-bouncing serves.

⌓ Strong eastern backhand returner
This grip will make it more difficult for an opponent to respond to low, wide balls.

⌓ Double-handed backhand grip
The most common backhand grip is the 50:50 grip in which the bottom hand is a continental grip and the top hand is an eastern forehand grip. The 50:50 is a versatile grip that allows your opponent to absorb power and make contact with the ball close to his body. His shots can be disguised well as a result. However, he may struggle to generate pace from balls hit at shoulder height and will have less reach out wide than with the single-handed backhand. (For more on double-handed grips, see pages 28–29.)

⌓ Eastern backhand grip
This is the most traditional single-handed backhand grip. It is a versatile grip that allows your opponent to deal effectively with low and wide balls. But he may struggle to generate pace and spin when hitting against a higher-bouncing ball.

⌓ Strong eastern backhand grip
A more extreme version of the eastern backhand grip that has evolved recently as players have had to deal with higher-bouncing balls and more topspin. Although effective when hitting balls with heavy topspin from between waist and shoulder height, it will potentially be more difficult for your opponent to deal with balls that are low and wide.

Your opponent's grip: exploiting the returning grip

Understanding what grip your opponent is using as he returns serve is a real advantage. An effective returner must be able to switch between forehand and backhand grips almost instantly – since he only has a split-second in which to perceive the direction of the oncoming ball. Certain grips restrict such a swift change, so simply serving to the opposite side can prove a great tactic.

Look out, too, for how your opponent uses his top hand when returning serve. The top hand is often used to aid the grip change between forehand and backhand returns. As soon as your opponent recognizes the direction of the serve, his top hand should tilt the racket towards the correct grip. If your opponent doesn't use his top hand in this way, then his grip change may take longer.

WHAT TO LOOK FOR

⌒ Semi-western forehand grip
This opponent is planning to return serve with a semi-western forehand. Note how his knuckles are placed beneath the grip and his hand has to move a long way around the racket to find a backhand grip. Serving with pace to his backhand side may prove effective.

⌒ Extreme eastern backhand grip
This opponent is holding a strong eastern backhand grip in readiness for returning serve. Again, his hand has to move a long way around the grip to find any kind of forehand grip, so serving to his forehand side may give you a real advantage.

⌒ Tilting towards forehand grip
Here, the top hand has helped to tilt the racket towards the forehand grip.

⌒ Tilting towards backhand grip
Here, the top hand has helped to tilt the racket towards the backhand grip.

TIP: identify extreme grips

Look out for players who use extreme grips to return serve. They will often be restricted with what they can do with their return.

Your opponent's grip: serving against the double-handed grip

One of the most effective grips with which to return serve is a double-handed grip. The extra hand on the grip provides more strength to deal with the speed of the oncoming ball, allowing your opponent to absorb its power and hit back with pace.

The double-handed grip also allows your opponent to make contact with the ball closer to his body – allowing a split-second longer to read the direction of the serve and prepare effectively. The return can also be disguised as it is hit with a shorter, punchier swing, which often doesn't give you any clues to its direction.

There are three main double-handed grips – each of which has the bottom hand in a different grip position.

For more advice on exploiting your opponent's grip: see page 27 (when you are serving); pages 70–73 (when you are attacking from the baseline); and pages 80–81 (when you are defending from the baseline).

The double-handed forehand

Although it is relatively rare to face an opponent with a double-handed forehand, many of the same serving principles apply. As with the double-handed backhand, the strength of the double-handed forehand return is that it can absorb the speed of an oncoming serve effectively. The big disadvantage of this grip is the lack of reach that comes with it.

WHAT TO LOOK FOR

Lack of reach
Look at the difference in reach between a single- and a double-handed forehand. As a server, it is crucial to be able to exploit this lack of reach by serving wide to the forehand effectively.

TIP: study the bottom hand

Glean as much information as possible about your opponent's double-handed grip. Although difficult to spot from the other end of the court, the position of his bottom hand often indicates the type of return that can be hit.

◔ 50:50 backhand grip
This is the most versatile double-handed grip available. The bottom hand is a continental grip and the top hand is an eastern forehand grip. It is called the 50:50 because both hands do an equal amount of work when hitting the ball.

◔ Take care with a 50:50 backhand returner
Using the versatile double-handed 50:50 backhand grip means that your opponent is more likely to be able to return serve comfortably.

∩ 25:75 backhand grip

➲ The 25:75 grip has the bottom hand holding the racket with an eastern forehand grip. This grip is often used by less experienced players who simply keep their forehand grip the same and add their other hand to the racket to form the backhand grip. The 25:75 grip is limiting because it is harder to create racket head speed and spin on the ball, and difficult to play against balls hit with width and pace. Some experienced players use the 25:75 grip in their returning stance, but switch to the 50:50 grip when they turn to play a backhand.

∩ Watch out for angled shots from a 25:75 backhand returner

The top hand is the dominant one (doing 75 per cent of the work). This means that your opponent can potentially create angles on his shots more easily.

∩ 75:25 backhand grip

➲ The 75:25 grip has the bottom hand holding a backhand grip and the top hand holding an eastern forehand grip. With this grip the bottom hand is dominant (doing 75 per cent of the work) and can generate lots of spin on the ball, although a wide ball can often expose it. When forced out wide, the top hand is often released from the racket during the follow-through. This lack of top-hand involvement may stop your opponent returning crosscourt.

∩ Serve wide to a 75:25 backhand returner

Your opponent will struggle to return a wide serve using the 75:25 double-handed backhand grip.

Your opponent's stance: when receiving serve

If you look carefully at your opponent's returning position, you will sometimes be able to spot the type of return he is planning to hit from the way he stands. The angle of his body can often give away the shot he will try to hit, no matter what type of serve comes at him.

↻ Hoping for a backhand

The angle of this opponent's body shows a leaning towards a backhand return. He will have to change his stance completely in order to hit a forehand return, so serving accurately down the middle of the court from the advantage side may cause him problems.

↪ Hoping for a forehand

The angle of this opponent's body shows him leaning towards a forehand return. This stance makes it easy for him to hit a forehand – a slight turn of the shoulders and he is ready to hit. He will have to make a far greater change to his position to hit a backhand return. Serving down the middle to his backhand from the deuce side could prove effective.

OPPONENT DISGUISING HIS STANCE

This opponent has disguised his stance: his grip remains neutral, allowing for a swift grip change if required, while the angle of his body doesn't give any clue as to the type of return he would prefer to hit. If he also takes up a central court position, then he will be able to cover both sides of the court equally well.

Your opponent's stance: on contact with the ball

As you serve, your opponent will move from his 'ready position' into a 'hitting position' just before making contact with the ball – giving you another chance to read the type of return you will face. Look at whether your opponent is about to hit on his front foot or back foot. This may indicate whether he is able to attack (front foot) or is more likely to defend (back foot). Consider also where his front foot is positioned on contact with the ball (i.e. a closed or open stance) for another clue as to the direction in which the return will be hit.

HITTING POSITION **WHAT TO LOOK FOR**

⋔ **Aggressive return on front foot**
When your opponent hits on his front foot, you'll need to be ready for an aggressive return (i.e. faster pace, deep or angled).

⋔ **Defensive return on back foot**
When your opponent hits on his back foot, the return is likely to be defensive (i.e. slower pace, shorter depth or less accurate).

POSITION OF FRONT FOOT **WHAT TO LOOK FOR**

⋔ **Closed stance**
The position of the front foot across the body (a 'closed' stance) makes it more difficult for your opponent to make contact with the ball far enough in front of his body, making it less likely that the return will be hit crosscourt.

⋔ **Open stance**
An 'open' stance (with the front foot positioned to the side of the back foot) allows the hips to rotate more easily, making a crosscourt return more likely (although you should be ready for all possible options).

2 USING VARIETY AS A WEAPON

The best servers are not always the ones who can hit the hardest – they are usually the ones who keep their opponents guessing as to where and how they will serve next.

Playing to your opponent's strength

Matching your serving strength to your opponent's returning weakness is obviously a great tactic, but there will be times when you will need to serve your least favourite serve to your opponent's favourite return. The question is, when?

Experienced players often choose to serve to their opponent's strength at the least important times in the match (for example, when 40–0 up). In this way, you are able to save your best match-up for the more crucial moments in the contest (when 30–40 down, for instance).

VARYING DIRECTION Even the most powerful of serves can be returned if your opponent knows in advance where it is heading – so being able to vary the direction of your serve is vital.

VARYING SPIN Changing the way in which the ball moves in the air and bounces off the court is another way of keeping your opponent guessing. More experienced players tend to use a combination of topspin (which kicks the ball higher than normal after the bounce) and slice (in which the ball stays lower than normal after the bounce). Using such a variety of spin on the ball creates trajectories that can be difficult for your opponent to track.

VARYING PACE If your serve isn't creating enough winning opportunities, then it may be time to increase its pace. This may mean you make more service errors, but it can still help you win more service games overall. Preventing your opponent from dominating you and gaining a mental advantage will be a positive step. From your opponent's perspective, hitting a winning return feels far better than just calling a serve out.

∩ Vary the direction
The angle of the racket face when it makes contact with the ball will ultimately determine the direction of your serve.

∩ Vary the spin
Throwing the ball slightly further to the left (for a right-hander) gives you the chance to hit with more topspin.

Disguising your serve

Try not to give away where you are planning to serve. Ideally, keep your pre-serve routine as consistent as possible. This means positioning yourself in the same place and maintaining the same look and feel to your service technique no matter what you intend to do with the ball.

Sometimes players inadvertently give away their intentions by preparing differently. For example, a player who bounces the ball more times than usual may be intending to hit harder than normal. A player may even look at the place where he is intending to serve – a big mistake! Try to avoid any such irregularities that could give your opponent any vital clues.

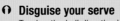

☊ **Adopt a neutral service position**
Using a neutral service position ensures that there is no way for your opponent to read in advance whether you are planning to serve down the middle, into his body or wide of him.

☊ **Disguise your serve**
Tossing the ball directly above your head when serving doesn't give your opponent a chance to read in advance the direction, pace or spin that you are going to put on the ball. This element of disguise on the serve is crucial; it maintains your ability to use variety as a real weapon. (For more information about reading your opponent's ball toss, see pages 52–53.)

CHECK YOUR DISGUISE

Find out how well you disguise your serve by asking your partner or coach to call out where he thinks you are about to hit the serve after you have thrown the ball into the air (but before you hit it). This will give you some great feedback. If your advisor can't tell from the other end of the court, ask him to stand behind you so he can take a closer look.

USING SERVING PATTERNS
TO YOUR ADVANTAGE

Think of the serve as the first shot in a sequence that continues to build pressure on your opponent and not just as a way to start the point. To do this you need to combine your serving strengths with your most effective shots from the baseline and the net as often as possible. This applies both to singles and doubles play.

Singles: serving wide from the deuce court

One of the most common serving patterns in singles is the wide serve hit from the deuce court with the server's second shot hit crosscourt into the space that has been created.

Player serving wide
The wide serve from the deuce court may be followed up by the server in one of three ways: either by hitting crosscourt, back behind the opponent or down the line (see opposite page).

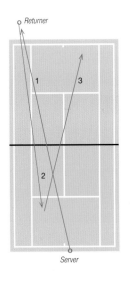

Returner

1   3

2

Server

⮕ Wide, then crosscourt

⮔ The wide serve (1) drags the opponent off the court – creating a big space crosscourt for the server's second shot to be hit into. In this example, the server has chosen to hit a groundstroke as his second shot (3). However, with a good enough serve this second shot could be a volley instead. This pattern can be executed no matter what direction the return is hit in.

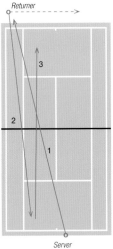

Returner

3

2

1

Server

⮕ Wide, then back behind

⮔ See here how the opponent has anticipated the server's second shot so quickly that he has inadvertently left a big space down the line instead. If you spot your opponent moving to cover his second shot too quickly in this way, then use the wrong-footing tactic of hitting the ball back behind him instead (3).

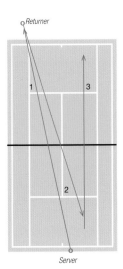

Returner

1   3

2

Server

⮔ Wide, then down the line

Here, the opponent has returned crosscourt (2), meaning that the server hits down the line (3) into the space rather than crosscourt. This is a slightly riskier second shot because it carries a lower margin of error (the down-the-line shot is hit over the higher part of the net and into a shorter court area). However, it is feasible as long as the server has control.

KEY THINGS TO CONSIDER

▶ **HOW DO YOU PLAY BEST?** Think about which serve will allow you to use your favourite shot from the baseline or net.

▶ **COMBINE YOUR STRENGTHS** In doubles, look to use the serve that combines the weapons of both you and your partner.

Singles: serving down the middle from the deuce court

You can use the serve down the middle of the court to create opportunities for slightly different patterns of play that can be just as effective as those resulting from the wide serve from the deuce court. The key thing to remember is that the middle serve keeps your opponent in a more central position – so less space is created naturally. Your opponent will often return a middle serve straight back down the middle of the court, so create an angle to your second shot by positioning yourself quickly around the ball.

Player serving down the middle
After serving down the middle from the deuce court, the server has two possible choices for his second shot: either hitting crosscourt or down the line (see opposite page).

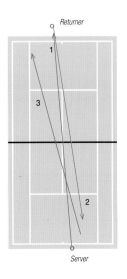

Returner

Server

➔ Middle, then crosscourt
↻ When the opponent's return drifts
back towards the server's forehand side (2), the server can hit his second shot crosscourt (3) to maintain pressure on his opponent.

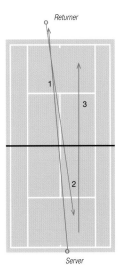

Returner

Server

➔ Middle, then down the line
↻ The same serve (1) is combined
with a strong forehand down the line instead of crosscourt (3).

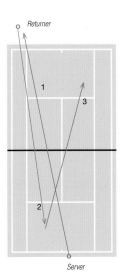

Returner

Server

↻ On the backhand side
The sequence of shots (above) can be repeated on the backhand side if the return is hit towards the server's backhand rather than forehand side. Remember that the central ball received from the opponent (2) requires the server to position himself well around the ball. This ability to create space around the ball is just as important as moving into a space to hit the ball.

TIP: anticipate the direction of the return
It is far more difficult for your opponent to return a good serve crosscourt because he needs to make contact with the ball further in front of his body. Therefore, when you know you have hit a strong serve, start anticipating the direction of the return in advance – giving you the chance to put even more pressure on your opponent.

Singles: serving wide from the advantage court

Using the wide serve to create a space for your second shot also applies from the advantage court. This playing pattern can be used to great effect by left-handed servers (using a sliced serve that swings wide and low), as well as right-handed servers who can use topspin to kick their serve high and wide of their opponent. Some right-handed players may find creating this angle more challenging, but it is important to do this if a right-handed opponent has a weak backhand return.

TIP: opt for a volley

All these winning serving patterns can be backed up by a volley rather than a ground-stroke, depending on the server's preference.

Player serving wide

After serving wide from the advantage court, the server has three possible options for his second shot: either hitting crosscourt, down the line or back behind his opponent (see opposite page).

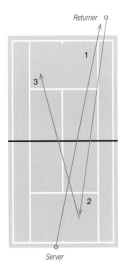

⮌ Wide serve, then aggressive ⮍ forehand crosscourt

A wide serve drags the opponent off the court (1) – creating a big space for the server to hit his second shot into. The server moves forwards to hit an aggressive forehand crosscourt (3).

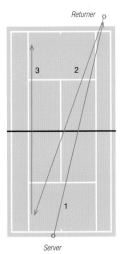

⮌ Wide serve, then ⮍ down the line

When the opponent's return is hit crosscourt (2), the server can hit his second shot down the line (3) instead of crosscourt.

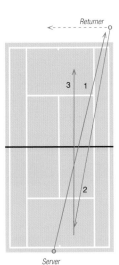

⮌ Wide serve, then back behind

⮍ Here, the opponent anticipates the server's second shot by moving across the court as soon as he has hit his return (2). This leaves a big space down the line behind the returner for the server to hit into comfortably (3).

Singles: serving down the middle from the advantage court

Although a favourite choice for right-handed servers, remember that there is less angle available for your second shot after serving down the middle from the advantage court. However, it is still a smart choice of serve when you are facing an aggressive right-handed opponent who has a dominant backhand return. It also carries a higher margin of error when compared to the wide serve because it is hit over the lower part of the net.

Player serving middle
After serving down the middle from the advantage court, the server has two possible options for his second shot: hitting crosscourt or down the line (see opposite page).

Returner

Server

↻ Down the middle, then
↺ backhand crosscourt

The server hits a strong serve down the middle of the court (1) and receives a crosscourt return to his backhand side (2). He then chooses to hit an aggressive backhand groundstroke crosscourt, which continues to build pressure on his opponent (3).

Returner

Server

∩ Down the middle, then
↻ backhand down the line

The same middle serve is hit (1) with the same return (2), but this time the server hits his backhand return down the line instead of crosscourt (3).

PRACTICE: test your serving patterns

Try this to test how well your serving patterns are progressing. Next time you play some practice points, tell your opponent where you plan to hit your first serve before every point. If you execute your patterns well enough, you'll be amazed at how many points you still win, even though your opponent knows where the ball is going.

Doubles: serving wide from the deuce court

For the right-handed player, the serve out wide from the deuce court can often be extremely effective – if the serve is hit with slice, it stays low and can drag an opponent wide of the court. Look how all three attacking patterns in the diagrams below have been executed successfully from the same serve direction. Remember that creating space with a wide serve is a great tactic as long as the serving team can remain in control of the rally.

TIP: doubles serving patterns

In doubles, there is less open court space to hit into. Therefore, agreeing specific patterns of play with your partner assumes an even greater importance. Knowing in advance where you plan to serve and position yourselves allows you to play more effectively as a team.

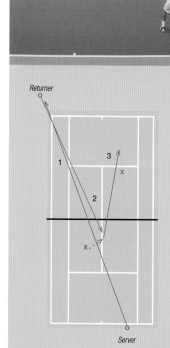

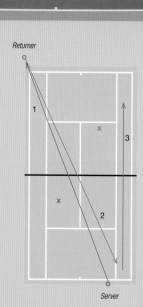

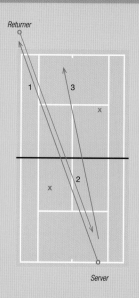

◖ Wide serve, then volley into space
A wide serve (1) allows the server's partner to intercept the return with a volley into the space between the opponents (3). The server's partner anticipates the direction of the return (2) – knowing that it is very difficult to return with an angle crosscourt from where the opponent is positioned.

◖ Wide serve, then aggressive down the line
In this situation the server hits an aggressive shot down the line (3) after serving wide (1). This is because the returner's partner has moved to a more central net position, creating a space down the line to hit into.

◖ Wide serve, then aggressive down the middle
Here, the server decides to hit an aggressive groundstroke down the middle of the court (3) because the wide serve (1) has created a big space between both the opponents.

Doubles: serving down the middle from the deuce court

Commanding the centre of the court is a key tactic in doubles, so serving down the middle is a natural choice for many experienced players. The weaker server also benefits from this choice because serving down the middle reduces the angles available to an opponent for an attacking return of serve.

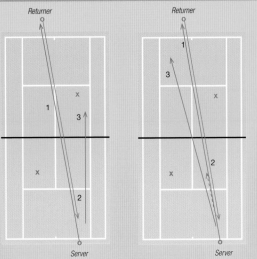

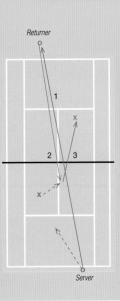

Down the middle, then attacking volley

The server's partner anticipates the weak return (2) and moves across the net to intercept with a winning volley (3). This intercept tactic can be planned before the point or left to the net player's judgment as to whether he moves across to volley or not – depending on the quality of the return. If it is planned before the point, then the server would automatically move into the space at the net left by his partner, who has moved across the net to hit the intercept volley.

Down the middle, then down the line

In the first diagram (above left) and the photograph, the net player leaves the ball from the return (2) for the server to attack with an aggressive groundstroke down the line (3).

Other options for the server's second shot include a lob down the line, a drop shot crosscourt to bring the returner deliberately in to the net, or an approach shot hit crosscourt so the server is able to join his partner at the net (shown in the second diagram above right).

Doubles: serving wide from the advantage court

This type of serve suits right-handed players who can hit with topspin (the kick after the bounce will move the ball even wider), as well as left-handed players who can hit with slice (the ball will stay low and wide after the bounce). A combination of second shots can be used depending on the playing preferences of the serving team and the weaknesses of their opponents.

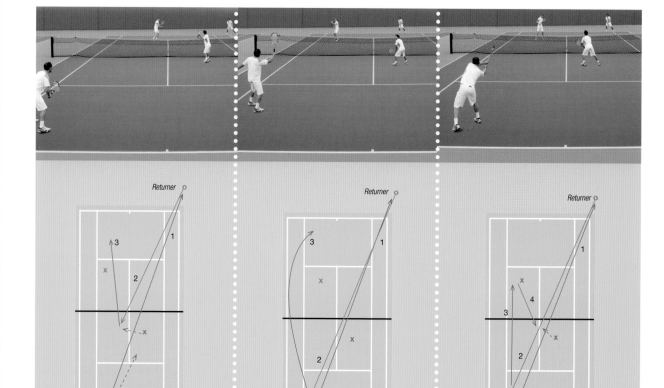

⋂ Wide serve, then volley into space

A wide serve (1) is backed up by the server's partner moving across the court and intercepting the return in the space between the opponents (3). This is a planned tactic, so the server automatically moves into the space left by his partner (who has moved across the net).

⋂ Wide serve, then lob down the line

This serving pattern involves the same serve out wide (1), but this time the server hits an aggressive lob over the opposing player at the net as a second shot (3). After the lob has been played, the server moves forwards to join his partner at the net to form a commanding position in the rally.

⋂ Wide serve, then hit at opponent

The server hits his second shot directly at the opponent at the net (3). See how the server's partner moves forwards diagonally in anticipation of a defensive volley being played by the net opponent (4).

Other second-shot options include a drop shot crosscourt (depending on the position of the returner) or an approach shot crosscourt.

Doubles: serving down the middle from the advantage court

Serving down the middle in doubles is a favourite for teams looking to use the serve-and-volley tactic. The middle serve allows them to take a more central net position – forcing their opponents to hit through them or over them in order to gain access to the net themselves.

↻ Serve to middle, then volley to feet

The middle serve (1) narrows the options available to the returner and allows the server's net partner to command the centre of the net. In this situation the net player intercepts the return (2) with a volley hit into the space between the opponents (3). The intercept volley tactic could be planned before the point or be played on instinct based on the quality of the return. See how the server moves to cover the position left by his partner at the net.

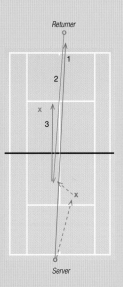

↻ Serve to middle, then crosscourt approach

The same middle serve has been hit (1), but this time the server hits the team's second shot as a crosscourt approach shot (3). The short return allows him to move forwards to join his partner at the net.

Other second-shot options include an aggressive groundstroke down the line, a lob down the line or a building groundstroke crosscourt that continues to pressurize the returner.

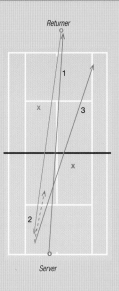

3

1 **Returning the first serve**

Neutralizing the threat of the first serve denies your opponent the opportunity to attack from the start. Gain an advantage immediately by looking closely at your opponent's grip, court position and ball toss.

See pages 48–53

returning serve

The return of serve is one of the most important shots in tennis because it needs to neutralize a strong serve or dominate a weak one. It is the ultimate test of your receiving skills since decision, movement and the execution of the shot all take place so quickly. A large part of returning well is the ability to anticipate how and where the serve will be played, alongside smart decisions about how you will counter it. This chapter will help you develop all these crucial tools for both singles and doubles.

2 Returning the second serve

The second serve will often be weaker than the first one, giving you a chance to gain a strong foothold in the rally. Learn how to return most effectively by both anticipating and influencing the type of serve you will face.

See pages 54–56

3 The return your opponent doesn't want you to hit

Discover which type of return will cause opponents most trouble based on the grip they use, their movement patterns and the court position they like to take up.

See pages 57–59

4 Using returning patterns to your advantage

Incorporating your return in a successful sequence of shots will help you win more often. This section looks at how you can do this best in both singles and doubles.

See pages 60–67

1 RETURNING THE FIRST SERVE

The first serve return can be one of the most difficult shots to play because you have to track the flight path of the ball speeding towards you and react almost instantly. Although the server remains in control of the shot there are some key visual clues that you can use to transform your reply into a real weapon.

The four main stages of service

There are four main stages to the serve: the ready position, the ball toss, contact and the finished position. The series of pictures on the right will give you an idea of what your opponent should look like at each stage. Note that the shoulder-over-shoulder rotation just before contact gives your opponent ultimate control over the placement of the ball, while the first two stages of the serve will give you the biggest clues as to where the ball will be hit.

GRIP Your opponent's grip will largely determine what she can do with her serve in terms of spin and pace. Less experienced opponents often use a grip that limits their options which, in turn, gives you a greater chance of anticipating the type of serve you will face (see page 50).

COURT POSITION The court position that your opponent serves from (i.e. where she positions herself along the baseline) will often give you clues as to the likely direction of her serve. This creates another opportunity to anticipate the serve and to stay one step ahead in the game (see page 51).

BALL TOSS An opponent's ball toss will often highlight where she won't be able to serve to. The position of the ball on contact with the racket is crucial in determining the direction, spin and pace of the serve. As a result, a less experienced opponent will often toss the ball into a position that only allows one or two types of serve to be hit – giving you a split-second advantage when facing a first serve (see pages 52–53).

🎧 **Ready position**

KEY THINGS TO CONSIDER

▶▶ **SPOT THE GRIP** Is the racket perpendicular to the ground or is it held at an angle?

▶▶ **OPPONENT'S POSITION** How close to the centre of the baseline is your opponent standing?

▶▶ **MEASURE THE TOSS** The wider the ball toss, the more your opponent's shot will be restricted in terms of direction, pace and spin.

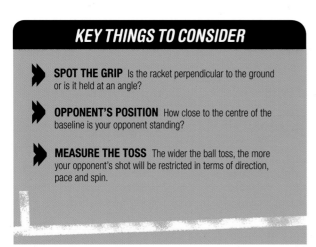

🎧 Ball toss　　　　　🎧 Contact!　　　　　🎧 Finished position

Reading your opponent's grip

How your opponent holds the racket when serving will often give you a clue to the type of serve you will face. Less experienced servers often use a forehand grip, which limits their options more than if they were to use a continental grip.

FOREHAND GRIP

A forehand grip allows an opponent to hit the ball hard and flat when serving but without significant topspin or slice. Although the serve can have power, it will often have very little spin, creating a very consistent serve that can be relatively easy to read.

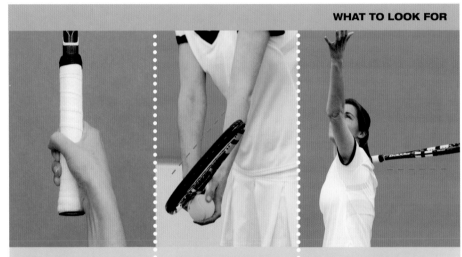

WHAT TO LOOK FOR

Ⓝ Grip giveaway
If the base knuckle of the server's index finger is resting on the flat side of the racket handle, then she is using a forehand grip.

Ⓝ Slanting racket edge
Is the racket edge slanted as the server is preparing to serve? This often indicates a forehand grip.

Ⓝ Horizontal racket face
Opponents who use a forehand grip to serve with will often point the hitting side of the racket face upwards.

CONTINENTAL GRIP

The continental grip is the recommended grip to serve with – it allows for power, spin and disguise. Players who use a continental grip will have far more options available to them when serving. From your point of view as a returner, it is important to recognize this grip as soon as possible, so at least you are prepared for the worst!

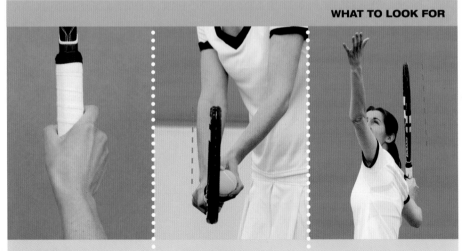

WHAT TO LOOK FOR

Ⓝ Shifted knuckle
If the base knuckle of the server's index finger is resting more towards the diagonal edge of the racket handle, then she is using a continental grip.

Ⓝ Perpendicular racket edge
If your opponent stands with the racket edge perpendicular to the ground, then she is probably using a continental grip.

Ⓝ Straight racket face
If the racket face points towards the side of the court, a continental grip is most likely being used.

Reading your opponent's court position

Where your opponent stands on the baseline can give you clues to the likely direction of her serve. For example, the closer the server stands to the centre of the baseline, the easier it is for the serve to be directed down the middle of the court. A wider position makes it easier to direct the serve wide because there is more angle available to her. Try to spot any obvious patterns that may arise from this positioning.

THE DEUCE COURT

MIDDLE FROM DEUCE COURT An opponent who stands in a central serving position when serving from the deuce court will be able to direct the ball straight down the middle of the court, no matter which grip she is serving with (1).

WIDE FROM DEUCE COURT An opponent who stands in a wider position will have more of an angle to hit an effective wide serve – particularly if she is using a forehand grip that prevents her from hitting with much spin (1).

THE ADVANTAGE COURT

MIDDLE FROM ADVANTAGE COURT Similar to the deuce court position, an opponent close to the middle of the court will be able to hit directly down the middle (1). Whether she can also hit wide from here depends on her grip and ball toss (see pages 52–53).

WIDE FROM ADVANTAGE COURT Taking a wider position to serve from on the advantage court gives the server more angle to play with when trying to serve out wide (1). Again, the grip and ball toss that she uses will also be a factor and you should look at these closely.

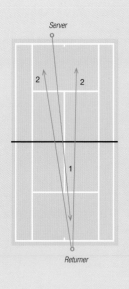

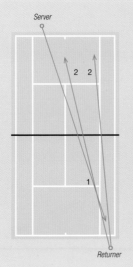

WHAT TO LOOK FOR

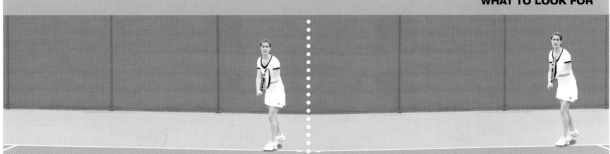

🎧 **Opponent serving from middle on deuce court**
If your opponent is serving from a central position, then it's more likely you'll have to deal with a serve straight down the middle of the court.

🎧 **Opponent serving from wide on advantage court**
If your opponent is standing wide on the advantage court to serve, then you may have to return a serve with a wider angle.

Reading your opponent's ball toss

The position of the ball when the racket makes contact with it is crucial in determining the direction, spin and pace of the serve. As a result, your opponent's ball toss will often give you vital clues about how and where the serve will be hit.

Ball tossed away from the body

If the ball is tossed too far away from the body the serve will often have excessive spin (slice) because the server has had to hit around the outside edge of the ball, making it very difficult to hit flat and straight. A right-handed server will often serve to the forehand of a right-handed returner with this ball-toss placement.

Ball tossed too far over the head

When the ball is tossed too far over the head, the server won't be able to maximize power. She will struggle to maintain her balance and often finish to the side of or behind the baseline – taking longer to recover for her next shot. Because of this, right-handed servers often have difficulty serving wide from the deuce court with this ball toss because they are forced into hitting the inside edge of the ball.

High ball toss

A high ball toss may make it difficult for the server to time her contact correctly (because she has to wait longer for the ball to drop). It may also produce more spin on the ball than normal (the racket may make contact with more of the underside of the ball). The important thing here is to be prepared for some inconsistent serving.

Low ball toss

A server with a very low ball toss will use a very quick service action because she lacks time to get into a fully extended throwing position. She will likely hit flat serves that fly low over the net (or into the net) because she hasn't been able to hit the ball at its highest point.

LOOK OUT FOR THE PERFECT BALL TOSS

The ideal placement for the ball is directly above and slightly in front of the server's head. (If it fell without being hit it would fall just in front of the server's nose.) This gives maximum power and control as she makes contact with the ball. Correct height also allows the server to hit the ball at full stretch for maximum power.

2 RETURNING THE SECOND SERVE

The second serve return brings a different tactical dimension to the game – here, the returner often wins most of the points since the server usually favours accuracy and consistency over power to ensure the ball isn't a fault. This is even true at a professional level, where servers often win less than half of all their second serve points.

Anticipating the type of serve you will face

You can increase your chances of successfully returning a second serve by paying close attention to your opponent's serving grip, as well as to the position of her back foot and hitting elbow. These will all give you vital clues to the type of serve you are about to face.

KEY THINGS TO CONSIDER

▶ **COUNTER YOUR OPPONENT'S STRENGTH** Use the middle of the court to neutralize your opponent's best serve and consider slowing the ball down and keeping it low if possible.

▶ **DOMINATE WHEN YOU CAN** Look out for a chance to attack your opponent's serve – especially a second serve.

SPOT THE SERVING GRIP An opponent using a forehand grip to serve will be severely limited in terms of what she can do with her second serve. The lack of spin that she can put on the ball means she will have to slow the pace of the serve down considerably (or take a big risk in hitting hard). Try to spot the angle of her racket face when serving. If using a forehand grip, she will often point the hitting side of her racket face upwards.

If the racket face points towards the side of the court, then she is more likely to be using a continental grip. The continental grip allows your opponent to use more pace, spin and disguise on her second serve.

WHAT TO LOOK FOR

🎧 **Opponent serving with forehand grip**
If your opponent's racket face is pointing upwards, then she will have limited options for what she can do on her second serve.

🎧 **Opponent serving with continental grip**
If the racket face is pointing towards the court side, your opponent is probably using a continental grip which will result in a more powerful second serve.

LOOK AT THE BACK FOOT You can often spot the likely direction of your opponent's second serve by looking at the position of her back foot just prior to contact with the ball.

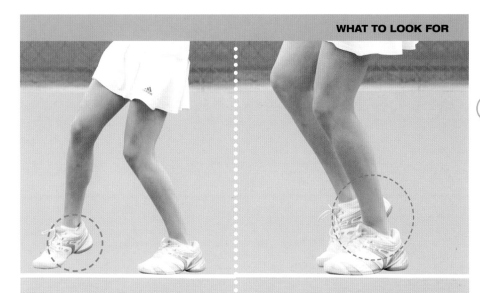

☊ **Back foot on baseline**
If the foot moves around the opponent's body and is placed on the baseline next to her front foot, the serve is likely to be hit with less power. This is because the server's upper body is starting to face forwards, preventing the shoulders from rotating over each other.

☊ **Back foot behind front foot**
Here, the server's feet are still aligned sideways – allowing her upper body to remain tilted and in a more sideways position. This allows the shoulders to rotate fully through the ball – so creating power and spin.

SPOT THE HITTING ELBOW Look out for the position of your opponent's hitting elbow. If it is positioned alongside her non-hitting elbow, then the serve will lack power. The back shoulder is no longer positioned behind the front shoulder – preventing sufficient upper-body rotation.

☊ **Elbow in front**
If the server's elbow is in front of her, then the serve will lack power.

☊ **Elbow behind**
If your opponent's hitting elbow is positioned behind her, then she has a far greater chance of serving effectively.

Influencing your opponent's serve

The second serve return will often allow you to gain an upper hand in the rally. Your opponent must hit the ball inside the service box – making it a guaranteed short ball. The server simply cannot afford to take risks with her second serve.

STEPPING IN One of the most effective ways to pressurize your opponent is by hitting the return of serve as early as possible from a position inside the baseline – at, or just after, the peak of its bounce. This gives the server less time to recover from the serve and prepare for the next shot, and gives you the chance to maintain an aggressive court position and generate pace on your return. Standing well inside the baseline to return serve may also intimidate your opponent enough into hitting a fault.

↻ **Return from inside the baseline**
Returning serve from well inside the baseline will enable you to make contact with the ball at its peak, allowing you to take time away from your opponent.

STEPPING ACROSS You can also influence your opponent by where you stand on the court. For example, leaving a bigger-than-normal space on your stronger forehand side may tempt her into serving there.

PRACTICE: knowing how early is early

Making contact with the ball at the peak of its bounce means hitting it exactly between the distance of its first and second (imaginary) bounce. Try placing markers where the serve's first bounce and second bounce land. You want to be making contact with the ball between the two. Often this position will be much further inside the baseline than you think.

⌒ **Leave some space**
Deliberately leave space on your forehand side for your opponent to serve into.

3 THE RETURN YOUR OPPONENT DOESN'T WANT YOU TO HIT

Experienced players combine high-quality shots with smart decision-making regarding where to hit their returns. Look at the playing style of your opponent after she has hit her serve to give you some great clues as to which type of return she would prefer not to face.

EXPLOITING THE SERVING GRIP Look out for the grip that your opponent uses to serve with. If she is using a forehand grip she may struggle to switch to a backhand grip if you put her under enough time pressure with your return. Simply hitting to her backhand side with speed may be enough to force her into an error. This applies in particular to opponents who use an extreme grip on either their forehand or backhand side because they will require a big change in grip after serving. (For more information on reading your opponent's serving grip, see page 50.)

THE MIRROR RETURN There are some returns that will always create problems for your opponent even before you know what her individual strengths and weaknesses are. One of these is the mirror return. This return is hit straight back to the opponent, 'mirroring' the direction of her serve. The advantage of this type of return is that it requires no decision – you simply hit the ball back where it came from. If this return is hit deep and fast enough, it will reduce the angle, space and time available for your opponent to hit her next shot.

WHAT TO LOOK FOR

◑ **No time to switch**
This opponent hasn't had time to switch grips and is trying to hit a backhand with her forehand grip. This will either result in an error or a very weak shot.

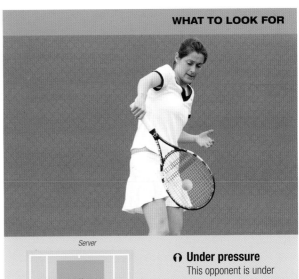

WHAT TO LOOK FOR

◑ **Under pressure**
This opponent is under time and space pressure.

◓ **Different mirror returns**
Play the mirror return (2) against any type of serve. The key to its effectiveness will be the depth and speed of the ball.

Server

2 2 2 2

Returner

THE SHORT-ANGLED RETURN This type of return challenges your opponent to move diagonally up the court, which can be a difficult type of movement since it requires a complex combination of perception, movement and preparation in a very short space of time. Players often prefer to move laterally (side-to-side) rather than diagonally because they often perceive the direction of the ball before its depth. So, when receiving a short-angled return, your opponent will tend to move across the court instinctively (recognizing direction) before moving forwards to the ball (recognizing depth). Moving in these two directions (instead of straight to the ball) is relatively inefficient.

Look out, too, for the side your opponent defends better with. For example, an opponent who uses a single-handed backhand slice will usually be able to defend better with this shot when she is pushed short and wide of the court compared to a double-hander.

WHAT TO LOOK FOR

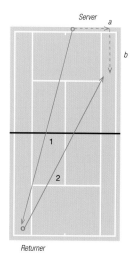

⋂ Hitting a short, wide ball
It is most likely that your opponent will hit a slower, higher ball from this position. If you see your opponent opening up her racket face to play a defensive shot, moving in to attack the next ball might be your best option. This opponent is struggling to reach a wide ball using a double-handed grip.

⟳ Direct movement
The serving opponent has moved straight to the ball (a).

Server

a

2

1

Returner

Server   a

b

1

2

Returner

⟳ Two-directional movement
This two-directional movement pattern (a and then b) has meant that the opponent has not reached the ball in time.

THE DROP-SHOT RETURN Hitting a drop-shot return is a great option if you see your opponent positioned deep behind the baseline after serving. After hitting a drop shot, moving forwards to anticipate a weak defensive shot is an excellent tactic if you sense your opponent will really struggle to reach the ball.

↻ Hitting a drop-shot return
Try to 'cushion' the ball slightly when you hit a drop-shot return. Absorbing the speed of the oncoming ball in this way allows you to control your shot so that you can hit with accuracy and precision.

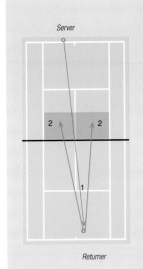

Server

2   2

1

Returner

➲ Drop-shot target area
↻ The target area for a drop shot doesn't have to be too close to the net because it is often the surprise element that beats your opponent. Aiming halfway between the service line and the net is often good enough (2).

In the photograph on the right, the serving opponent is scrambling to reach the ball after the returning player has hit a drop-shot return. The returner will move forwards if she senses her opponent is under pressure.

Playing a specific sequence of shots, which starts from the return of serve, will give you great confidence as a player. These patterns of play are often used by experienced players depending on the type of serve – and opponent – they are facing.

Singles: neutralizing a strong first serve

You can use effective patterns of play even against a very strong server. To do this effectively, you need to make neutralizing your opponent's dominance your first priority. Many less experienced players struggle to do this. Instead, they try to attack straight away – making a high number of errors in the process.

SLOWING THE PACE Reducing the speed of the return can help to neutralize the server's threat immediately. Big servers often like to back their serve up with an aggressive, pacy groundstroke. Some of this pace comes from the ball you hit back.

The blocked return allows you to hit a controlled ball back to your opponent without giving her much pace to work with. The action is similar to a volley – simply cut down your swing and make contact with the ball in front of your body. This simple action can be relatively easy to time against a fast serve.

↻ Use a forehand blocked return
Make contact with the ball in front of your body and hit with a touch of slice on the ball. Both these factors will help you take pace off the ball and keep the bounce low when it reaches your opponent.

KEY THINGS TO CONSIDER

 SWITCH YOUR POSITION Try changing your court position to counter a very strong serve from your opponent.

 OPPONENT TOO CLOSE? In doubles, try to spot how close your opponent is to the net since the lob may be a great option for you.

THE LOWER THE BETTER Keeping your return low when facing a strong first serve will often make it harder for your opponent to attack with her next shot. The low return, no matter where it is hit on the court, forces your opponent into hitting up over the net and gives you a split-second longer to recover. This tactic is particularly effective against opponents who use a big backswing and/or extreme grip.

➲ Keep the ball low
The low bounce of this return will challenge your opponent if she is using a big, high backswing. The height of the ball makes it much harder for her to attack with her next shot.

MIDDLE, THEN SPACE
Returning down the middle of the court is a great option because it immediately reduces the angle available for your opponent's next shot. Experienced players often look to neutralize by hitting down the middle of the court with their return before stepping up to attack wide of centre once momentum has swung back in their favour.

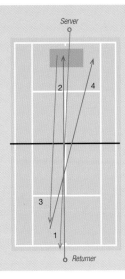

Server

Returner

↻ Achieving middle, then space
The shaded part is the target area for the deep, middle return to be played into. Note how the returner plays here first (2) before hitting her second shot into more space (4). This sequence can be used against any type of serve.

PRACTICE: neutralizing first serves

During practice, only play the point out if you feel you have neutralized well enough with your first serve return. Aim to get back to at least a 50:50 position in the rally – otherwise the point stops immediately.

Singles: building patterns against a weak second serve

The second serve return is a great way to pressurize your opponent immediately. However, you also need to use a sequence of shots after your return that maintain and build on your momentum in the rally. Unlike when facing a strong first serve, returning a weak second serve immediately into the space on the court can be a real advantage. Pushing your opponent wide, deep or short of the court allows you to open up opportunities to attack.

THE DROP-SHOT RETURN Deciding where to position yourself after hitting a drop-shot return is crucial. Move forwards if you see your opponent really struggling to reach the ball because it is likely she will only manage a short reply. The next shot can often be volleyed away for a winner. If you sense that your drop shot hasn't put your opponent under enough pressure, positioning yourself just inside the baseline is a good option.

TWO-SHOT PATTERNS OF PLAY

ATTACKING FROM THE DEUCE COURT

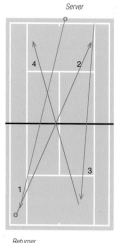

Server

Returner

↻ Crosscourt attack
Attack crosscourt with a forehand return (2) and then aggressively crosscourt with a backhand (4). Hitting to two opposite spaces in quick succession like this is a great tactic.

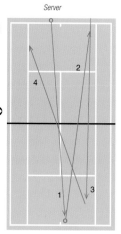

Server

Returner

Inside-in attack ↻
Attack with a backhand inside-in (down the line) (2) before hitting aggressively crosscourt with a forehand (4). Note how the returner here has to create the space more to attack into from this position.

ATTACKING FROM THE ADVANTAGE COURT

Server

Returner

↻ Two-space pattern
Use a two-space pattern by attacking crosscourt with a backhand return (2) and then crosscourt with a forehand groundstroke (4).

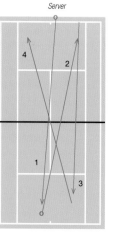

Server

Returner

Inside-out attack ↻
If you favour your forehand, attack with an inside-out forehand return (a forehand hit crosscourt from the backhand side of the court) (2) and then with a forehand crosscourt groundstroke (4).

⟳ Ready for anything
This player's position just inside the baseline allows her to move easily either forwards or backwards.

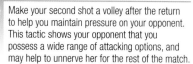

TIP: volley as second shot

Make your second shot a volley after the return to help you maintain pressure on your opponent. This tactic shows your opponent that you possess a wide range of attacking options, and may help to unnerve her for the rest of the match.

THE CHIP AND CHARGE You may approach the net after hitting a slice return down the line or down the middle of the court. Even if your opponent anticipates this tactic, there is still enormous pressure on her to pass or lob you once you are positioned at the net. Players with strong sliced backhands often use this pattern to great effect.

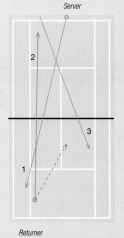

Server

Returner

Down-the-line approach

Note how the down-the-line approach (2) forces the serving opponent into creating an angle crosscourt in order to hit past the net player (3). This can be a very difficult shot to hit when under pressure.

In the photograph on the left, the returning player hits a slice backhand return down the line before moving forwards to cover the net.

THE AGGRESSIVE LOOP An alternative way of approaching the net is the aggressive loop. This type of return is hit high over the net with heavy topspin. The extra time it takes to reach your opponent gives you the chance to take up a strong net position. The aggressive loop is particularly effective against an opponent who struggles to deal with a high-bouncing ball.

High bounce to backhand

This player has hit an aggressive backhand return crosscourt with heavy topspin. The high bounce of the ball pushes her opponent deep behind the baseline, enabling the player to approach the net effectively.

PRACTICE: restrict your shots

Allow yourself only three shots in total to win the point when returning a second serve (a maximum six-shot rally). If you need more, you lose the point automatically. This will help you focus on your very best shots right away.

Doubles: neutralizing a strong first serve

The use of returning patterns is important in doubles because the lack of space on the court requires a team to plan their shots very carefully. The principle of reducing the available angles on the court when facing a strong serving team remains crucial, and there are a number of ways in which you can do this.

BOTH BACK A really effective way of neutralizing the dominance of a strong first serve in doubles is for both players to take up a baseline position when returning. This can change the whole look of the court to the server – and, crucially, takes away a net target for the opposition to aim at.

DEFENSIVE NET POSITION Returning teams who don't want to give up their net position immediately may choose to maintain a normal one-up/one-back formation, but with a more defensive slant. This means the returner's partner stands just behind the service line, with a view to moving forwards after a strong return, or moving backwards after a weak return.

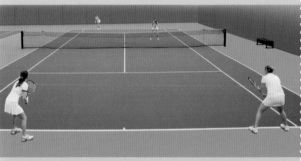

◖ **Both on the baseline**

➲ Because both players are positioned on the baseline there is no longer an obvious net player for the serving team to aim at. This tactic is useful for returning teams who rely on strong groundstrokes. It can also be effective on slower-bouncing courts (such as clay courts) where it is more difficult to put the volley (3) away for a winner.

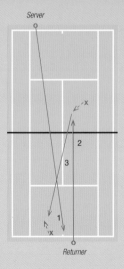

◖ **One-up/one-back**

➲ The returner's partner angles her body so that she can quickly read the type of return that will be played. This allows her to make a quick decision on whether to move forwards or backwards.

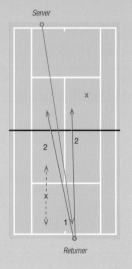

DEFENDING WITH THE LOB

The lob is an excellent return to play under pressure because it buys you and your partner time to reposition yourselves, and can cause confusion to an opposing team if hit in the right place.

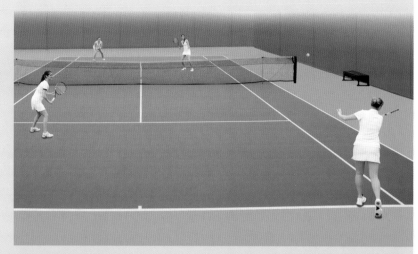

⌒ Lob down the line
↻ Hitting over the head of the opposing net player (down the line) is a great choice – especially if the server follows her serve in to the net (2). This forces both the server and her partner to change positions quickly.

DEFENDING WITH THE BLOCKED RETURN

Slowing the pace of the ball by using a blocked return allows you a split-second longer to recover and plan what your next shot will be. The blocked return is an effective shot as long as you can direct the ball away from the opposing net player (the pace of the ball makes it quite easy to volley against). It is also an excellent choice of shot to play against a server who decides to follow her serve in to the net.

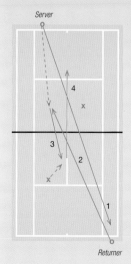

↻ Blocking to the feet
⊃ Block down to the feet of the incoming server (2) to force her to hit her first volley high over the net (3). This creates a potential attacking situation for your team.

If you find yourselves being dominated too often by a team serve-and-volleying, planning to intercept the server's first volley is a momentum-changing tactic. Your partner must move across the net to intercept the first volley of the server (4). Although a high-risk strategy, this tactic can totally throw a serving team off their rhythm.

Doubles: building patterns against a weak second serve

Building pressure with a second serve return is as important in doubles as it is in singles. Using specific returning patterns will give you and your partner the chance to take control of the court – both from the baseline and the net.

ATTACKING CROSSCOURT Returning aggressively crosscourt opens up a number of offensive options for the returning team. Joining your partner at the net by approaching behind her return allows you to take command of the front of the court. Hitting the return deep and wide of the court will make it very difficult to pass or lob you as long as you are positioned correctly. The key to good positioning is to move together – following the line of the ball you have just hit. This shoulder-to-shoulder movement prevents any big gaps appearing between you. (For more on this, see page 96.)

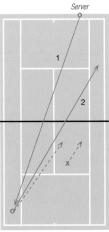

⟳ Deep wide return
⟳ Hit a deep wide return (2), which will allow you to approach the net. Both you and your partner then follow the line of the ball and move diagonally forwards.

⟳ Short-angled return
⟳ Play a short-angled return (2) and then approach the net. Again, your team moves forwards in order to anticipate the opposing team's scrambled reply.

ATTACKING DOWN THE LINE

A weak second serve will also create an opportunity to attack down the line. Knowing in advance that you are planning to hit down the line for your next shot enables your partner to anticipate a weak return from the opposing net player.

ATTACKING WITH THE LOB

Another way to approach the net as a returner is by using the lob over the head of the opposing net player. This allows you to move forwards to join your partner at the net. Unlike the first serve return, you may be positioned further inside the baseline to return the second serve, so remember you have less space to hit into from here.

INTERCEPTING BALL 3
Just as you might plan to serve and volley, you can also plan for your partner at the net to use an intercept volley against the server's second shot. Play an aggressive return crosscourt that puts pressure on the server – forcing her into a defensive second shot. Your partner then moves across the net to intercept this shot with a volley down to the feet of the opposing net player.

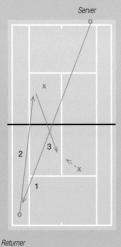

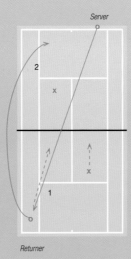

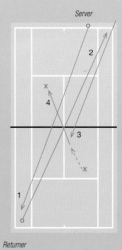

◓ Central intercept
The returner's partner moves more centrally in anticipation of a weak volley (3) after the aggressive return down the line has been played (2).

◓ Lob from inside baseline
A lob played from inside the baseline (2) gives you less space to hit into compared with a lob played from behind the baseline. However, it is still an effective tactic to use if hit with enough control.

◓ Intercept volley
Return aggressively crosscourt from the advantage court (2). This forces the server deep and wide of the baseline (3). The target area for the intercept volley is down to the feet, or just behind, the opposing net player (4).

◓ Communicate
The key to using effective returning patterns is based on partners communicating well with each other. Knowing what your partner is most likely to do next gives you the chance to anticipate your own next move. This proactive approach helps maintain feelings of control and confidence – whether you are the underdog or the favourite to win.

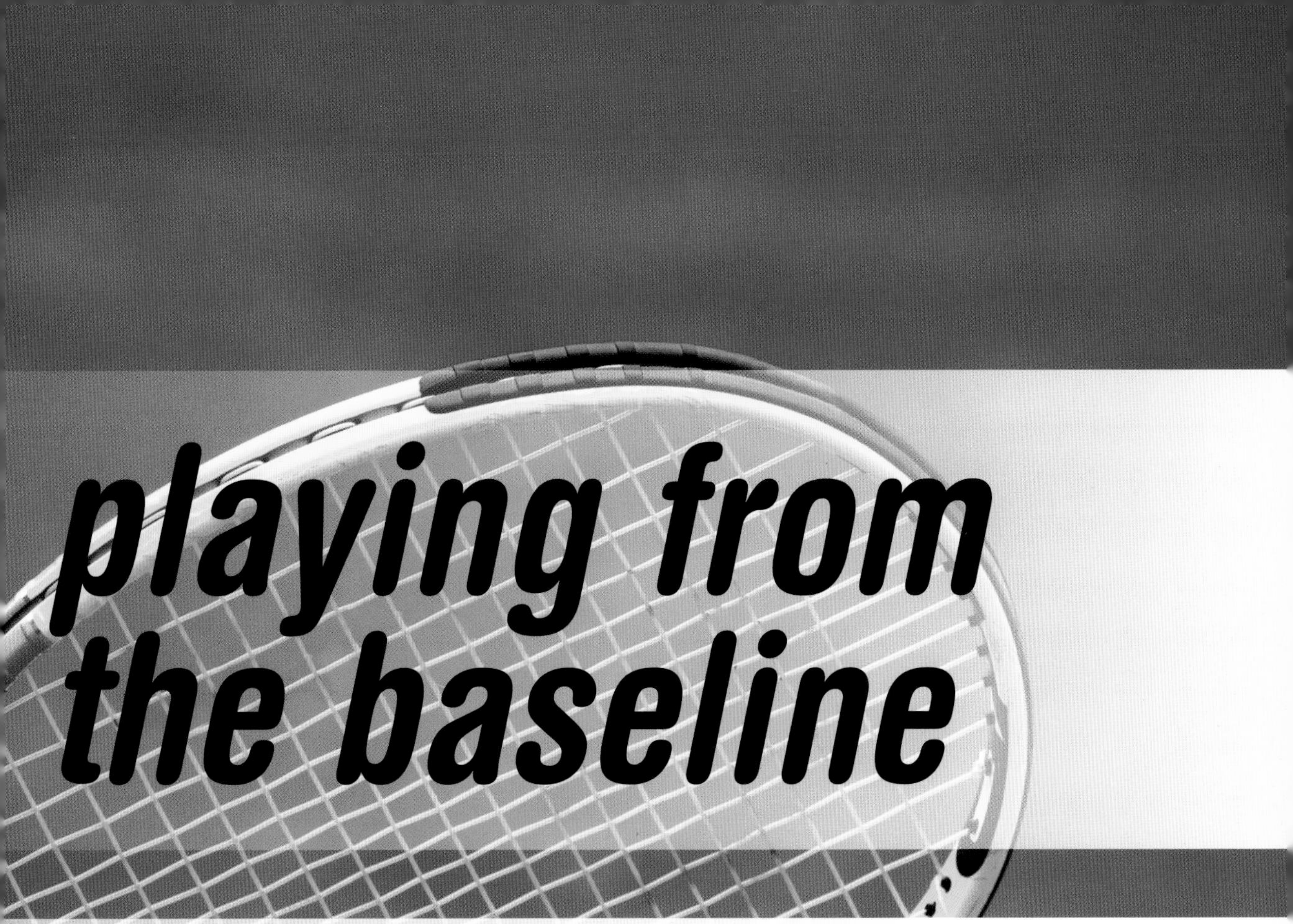

playing from the baseline

At any point during a baseline rally you will find yourself either attacking, defending or trading. This chapter looks at all three tactical options in detail and suggests ways to spot your opponent's next move by looking at his grip, swing shape and court position. It also recommends successful patterns of play to use from the baseline when you are playing both singles and doubles.

1 Attacking from the baseline

Find the best method of attack from the baseline by looking at where your opponent will be weakest. And then learn how to combine your favourite shots into a successful pattern of play.

See pages 70–79

2 Defending from the baseline

Learn about the best court position to defend from and what clues will give away how your opponent is planning to attack. This section also provides specific defensive playing patterns to help you get back into a rally when you're under pressure.

See pages 80–85

3 Trading from the baseline

This section will show you how to play more effectively when there is an equal balance of play between you and your opponent. This means playing with both consistency and cleverness, which will enable you to gain an advantage later on in the rally.

See pages 86–87

1 ATTACKING FROM THE BASELINE

Attacking an opponent from the baseline can be done using a combination of ball characteristics – height, direction, depth, speed and spin. The way you attack should also reflect the playing style and preference of your opponent. Your opponent's grip, swing shape and court position will all influence how, when and where you attack.

Exploiting your opponent's grip

There are certain types of shot that your opponent won't want to face when you attack him from the baseline. His ability to defend against you will be strongly influenced by the forehand or backhand grip that he is using.

For more advice on exploiting your opponent's grip: see page 27 (when serving); pages 28–29 (when serving against double-handed grips); and pages 80–81 (when you are defending from the baseline).

↻ Strong baseline attack
Attacking effectively from the baseline often requires you to employ specific strengths against your opponent's weaknesses.

YOUR OPPONENT'S FOREHAND GRIP

↻ Continental grip
Although potentially more effective when being attacked with fast, low balls, using this grip will make it very difficult for your opponent to deal with higher-bouncing balls (above shoulder height); balls that bounce very deep in the court; or balls that bounce very close to the body (the ideal contact point is away from the body).

↻ Ball too close for opponent
It will be very difficult for your opponent to neutralize the ball effectively using a continental grip when the ball is hit so close to his body.

Eastern forehand grip

This common forehand grip will potentially be more effective for your opponent if you attack him with wide and low balls. However, the grip will make it more difficult for him to deal with higher-bouncing balls (i.e. those above shoulder height), as well as balls that bounce very deep in the court. This grip is often used on faster court surfaces with lower bounces (such as indoor carpet courts, artificial grass courts and real grass courts).

Semi-western forehand grip

One of the most versatile grips, many experienced players use it on their forehand side. It can be adapted to various contact points and will enable your opponent to defend from a variety of positions. Although your opponent will find it more difficult to defend against balls bouncing above shoulder height, you should also test him low and wide to discover his weakest position. Take note of his swing shape and court position to gain a better insight into possible weaknesses.

Western forehand grip

The most extreme type of forehand grip in use. It is typically used by players who play on high-bouncing courts (such as clay courts). It will prove most effective for your opponent when used to return high balls because the ideal contact point will be higher and closer to his body than with other grips. However, he won't like being attacked short, low and/or wide of the court with pace.

Ball too high for opponent

Your opponent will struggle to deal with height on a ball. He will be unable to create enough spin and pace from this contact point. (The eastern forehand grip is more effective from a lower height.)

Ball too wide for opponent

A grip change is needed for a backhand, so attacking with a wide ball to your opponent's forehand and then backhand side in quick succession could prove effective.

Ball too low and wide for opponent

Exploit the disadvantages of the western forehand grip – it's most limiting when your opponent has to deal with pacy short, low or wide shots.

YOUR OPPONENT'S BACKHAND GRIP

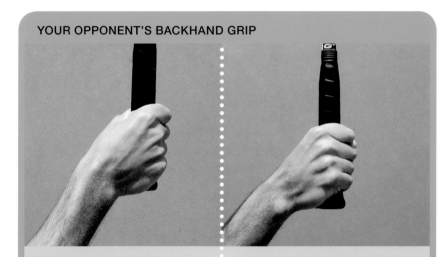

∩ Eastern backhand grip

The eastern backhand is probably the most common single-handed grip in use. It will allow your opponent to make a comfortable switch between topspin and slice, as well as to other grips for the serve, forehand and volley. Potentially very effective when defending against low and wide balls, so try to challenge your opponent with higher-bouncing balls.

∩ Strong eastern backhand grip

This is a more extreme version of the eastern backhand grip and is favoured by players who play on high-bouncing courts. It is most effective for your opponent on high balls because the ideal contact point is higher and closer to his body than with other grips. However, your opponent will need to make a big change to find a forehand grip, so attacking to the backhand and then forehand side in quick succession can make for a winning combination.

∩ Ball too high and deep for opponent

Your opponent may struggle to produce enough power and control against high, deep balls.

∩ Ball too low and wide for opponent

Your opponent won't like being attacked short, low and/or wide of the court with pace when using a strong eastern backhand.

KEY THINGS TO CONSIDER

 SPOT THE GRIP Is your opponent using an extreme grip for his groundstrokes? If so, which shot will trouble him most?

 MEASURE THE SWING How big is your opponent's backswing?

 MIX AND MATCH Which is your best two-shot combination from the baseline?

YOUR OPPONENT'S DOUBLE-HANDED BACKHAND GRIP

Double-handed 50:50 grip

Here, the bottom hand is a continental grip and the top hand an eastern forehand grip. This versatile grip allows your opponent to absorb power and make contact with the ball close to his body. Shots can be disguised well, and the grip will prove effective for your opponent on passing shots, so put him under pressure if you are attacking this grip with an approach shot.

Your opponent may struggle to generate pace from balls hit at shoulder height. This grip also gives him less reach out wide than a single-handed backhand.

Double-handed 25:75 grip

This grip has the bottom hand holding the racket with an eastern forehand grip. It is often used by inexperienced players who keep their forehand grip the same and then add the other hand to the racket to form a backhand grip.

The dominance of the top hand enables your opponent to create angles with his defensive shots. But the 25:75 grip will also make it harder for him to create racket-head speed and spin on the ball when he is being attacked. This grip is also difficult to use against balls that are hit with width and pace.

Double-handed 75:25 grip

This grip has the dominant bottom hand in an eastern backhand grip (doing 75 per cent of the work) and the top hand in an eastern forehand grip.

Your opponent will be able to create lots of topspin and be more comfortable dealing with higher-bouncing balls. He will struggle with wide balls, while the lack of involvement of the top hand will make defending crosscourt more difficult. The bigger grip change required between forehand and backhand means attacking to alternate sides in quick succession may prove successful.

Ball bouncing too high for opponent

Your opponent may struggle to defend against a high ball if he is using a 50:50 double-handed backhand grip.

Ball too wide and pacy for opponent

An opponent using a 25:75 double-handed backhand grip will be challenged by balls that bounce wide with pace.

Challenge the crosscourt backhand

Break a 75:25 double-handed backhand grip by forcing your opponent to defend crosscourt as the top hand is less involved.

Exploiting your opponent's swing

Your opponent's grip will directly affect the type of swing shape and position that he uses when defending from the baseline. You will be able to pick up some great visual clues as to what type of shot he is attempting to hit by looking closely at this setup position.

ATTACKING TO THE FOREHAND SIDE Opponents who use big swings on their forehand side in order to hit with power, depth and spin will usually employ more parts of their body when making their shot. This creates a longer and more complex chain of movements, and can potentially be challenged with balls hit to them with power.

Opponents who use small swings on their forehand will be able to time the ball better as their swings are simpler and use fewer parts of their body. This means they will be able to deal with pacy shots more easily. However, they'll be challenged when defending against higher-bouncing balls and when being attacked from deep court positions because their swing won't generate enough power from these positions.

Looking at your opponent's position as he is about to hit the ball will also help. For example, opponents who hit their forehand with their front leg across their back leg (referred to as a closed stance) will struggle to hit the ball crosscourt when you put them under pressure. This is because their contact point will often not be far enough in front of their body.

⌒ Closed stance
Your opponent will struggle to hit crosscourt from this position, so the ball is more likely to be hit down the middle or down the line.

⌒ Big backswing
Opponents using a big backswing will struggle to get into the correct hitting position in time against a fast-paced ball.

⌒ Small backswing
This opponent will struggle to deal with the height of the ball because his backswing is too short and low.

ATTACKING TO THE BACKHAND SIDE Opponents will defend in very different ways depending on whether they are using a single- or double-handed backhand. For example, single-handed players tend to defend with more slice on their backhand side than topspin. This is because the swing is shorter and can absorb the pace of the oncoming ball more efficiently. The double-hander, on the other hand, will usually use the strength of both hands to absorb your attack and will hit back with topspin more often.

ATTACKING A SINGLE-HANDER

WHAT TO LOOK FOR

Try to attack an opponent who uses a single-handed topspin backhand with pace as often as possible. This is because the single-handed backhand is a more precise shot, requiring your opponent to make contact in front of his body more than if he were to hit the ball with two hands.

◑ Hitting late
This opponent is struggling to deal with the pace of the oncoming ball because he hasn't been able to make contact in front of his body in time.

◑ Slice backhand
You will often see opponents playing with slice when under pressure on their backhand side. Expect the ball to be played back slower and with a lower bounce. This defensive slice will often float over the net, which means you may be able to move in to volley against it.

ATTACKING A DOUBLE-HANDER

WHAT TO LOOK FOR

Opponents who defend with a double-handed backhand will find it difficult to deal with balls that are hit wide of them. This is because their reach to the ball is much shorter compared with the single-hander.

⮕ One hand off
If you see your opponent taking one hand off his grip, then this usually means his shot will be hit without much pace.

Singles: attacking patterns of play

How and where you attack is determined by your playing style and preferences, as well as how your opponent plays. Therefore, it is important to be able to combine your strengths into repeatable patterns of play as often as possible when you're playing both singles and doubles (see pages 78–79).

Many successful patterns of play start from an attacking serve or return. However, there will be times when these two shots fail to change the momentum in the rally. In this situation, look for opportunities to attack your opponent as the rally progresses, and base your decision on your own positioning as well as that of your opponent.

ATTACKING DOWN THE LINE Perhaps the most common way to attack from the baseline is to rally crosscourt before attacking down the line. To do this effectively, your crosscourt shots need to build a position of strength in the rally first. This usually means hitting consistently deep or wide enough to force your opponent into hitting shorter and softer.

ATTACKING CROSSCOURT There will be times when attacking crosscourt is the best option. This will often be when your opponent has anticipated you hitting down the line. When you spot your opponent moving across the baseline too early, hitting back behind him crosscourt is a great shot to play.

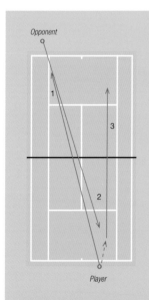

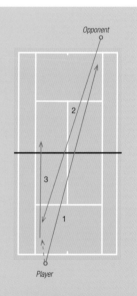

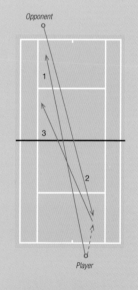

⋒ **Build, then attack down the line**

Hit a deep crosscourt forehand (1), forcing your opponent into hitting short (2). Next, move forwards to attack down the line with a forehand (3). Note how the target for the down-the-line shot is not as deep as the crosscourt target. This is because the change of direction and increased speed of the ball is enough to pressurize your opponent.

⋒ **Build, then attack with a drop shot**

This player hits a drop shot down the line (3) after hitting a deep crosscourt backhand (1). Unlike the deeper down-the-line shot in the first diagram (above left), the shorter depth serves to beat the opponent.

⋒ **Build, then attack back behind**

If your opponent moves across the baseline too early, he will leave a big space crosscourt for you to hit back into (3).

⋒ **Deep, then short**

This player has used a two-ball combination of forehands by first hitting a deep crosscourt shot (1) and then a short-angle crosscourt shot (3). The angle of the second shot forces his opponent extremely wide of the court.

Singles: counter-attacking patterns of play

Counter-attacking tactics are used by players who enjoy recycling the pace of their opponents' shots in order to attack them back. They are often used by players with shorter swings (who can't generate their own pace that well), as well as by players who have a particularly strong shot that they hit well while moving across the baseline.

THE DELIBERATE SPACE A classic counter-attacking tactic is to leave a deliberate space open for your opponent to hit into. For example, a player who loves to hit his forehand on the run will deliberately rally with his backhand crosscourt and remain positioned on the backhand side of the court – tempting his opponent into hitting down the line to his forehand side.

∩ Use your
⮌ favourite shot
Tempt your opponent into hitting down the line (2), so allowing you to move across the baseline and hit a favourite forehand crosscourt (3) on the run.

THE TRADING SWITCH Using the trading switch (by changing the direction of your shot) is a great way of forcing your opponent into playing to your baseline strength. We know that the vast majority of shots hit down the line will be hit back crosscourt. Therefore, hitting a neutral ball down the line from your weaker side will lure your opponent into hitting crosscourt back to your favoured side (see also page 86).

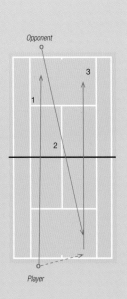

⮌ Down-the-line trade
Hit a backhand down the line (1) in order to force your opponent into hitting back crosscourt (2) to your forehand strength. Hitting slightly slower and higher will also give you more time to move across the court for your next shot.

THE SLOW BALL Mixing up the pace of your shots is another great way of frustrating your opponent. Using a two-ball combination of shots, first slow and then fast, can often work well.

∩ Slow/fast combo
This player uses his backhand slice (above left) to slow the ball down and bring his opponent inside the baseline before hitting aggressively with his topspin backhand in order to pressurize with speed and depth (above right).

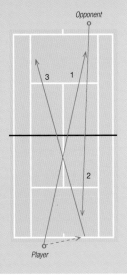

Doubles: attacking patterns of play

The most common form of baseline play in doubles is when both pairs are in a one-up/one-back formation. In other words, the server and returner are exchanging baseline shots crosscourt with both partners positioned at the net. There are a number of ways to attack from this situation.

BUILDING GROUNDSTROKE, FINISHING VOLLEY One of the key jobs of the baseline player is to create opportunities for his partner to intercept with a volley at the net. Therefore, hitting consistently crosscourt with depth and width is a surefire way to involve your partner.

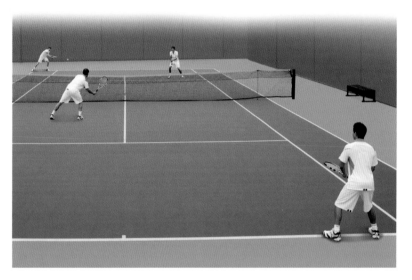

ATTACKING DOWN THE LINE

This is a great option if you spot your opponent at the net moving across the court too early to intercept a crosscourt groundstroke. Double-handed players in particular can disguise the down-the-line shot really well because they can afford to make contact with the ball a little later than the single-hander. Even if your net opponent doesn't move from his position, hitting straight at him when the ball is short is another strong play.

◑ Creating chances
In doubles, the baseline player is often the one who creates chances for attacking net play. See how the opponent's defensive shot may be intercepted by the player at the net.

◐ Strong forehand crosscourt
The baseline player plays a strong forehand crosscourt (1), forcing his opponent deep and wide of the court (2). This allows his partner to move forwards and intercept with a finishing volley at the net (3).

◑ Attacking at opponent
Attack down the line straight at your opponent at the net (2). Note how the player's partner at the net also moves in towards the net opponent in anticipation of a short, weak volley (3).

LOBBING DOWN THE LINE The aggressive lob is particularly effective when your net opponent is standing very close to the net or when you are pushed deep behind the baseline but remain in control of your shot.

On the other hand, when the oncoming ball lands very short (closer to the service line than the baseline), using the lob down the line may not be your best option. This is because you need a certain amount of space to lob into (especially if you don't hit with much spin). In these cases, a very short ball should be attacked with an aggressive groundstroke rather than a lob.

Even if you end up losing the point, hitting down the line with a pass or a lob will make your opponent more wary about intercepting in the future. This may make hitting crosscourt easier for you for the rest of the match.

Doubles: counter-attacking patterns of play

Counter-attacking tactics are used by doubles players who are more comfortable hitting groundstrokes from the baseline than hitting volleys at the net. They use a both-back formation (i.e. both players are positioned on the baseline).

The strength of this formation is that opponents often don't know where to hit their volleys and smashes. If they have no targets at the net to aim for, the opposing team will often try too hard to create winning spaces and angles that may not even exist.

Both-back formation
This formation is especially effective for doubles players who favour baseline play over net play.

In the photograph above, the both-back formation shows there is no longer an obvious volley target for the opponent at the net to aim for.

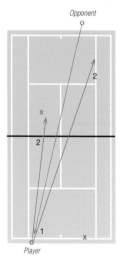
Opponent

Player

Effective lob
This player has used the lob effectively (2); his net opponent is positioned extremely close to the net, which means that the biggest space on the court is behind him.

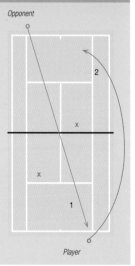
Opponent

Player

2 DEFENDING FROM THE BASELINE

The key to good defensive play is to try to neutralize your opponent's threat as soon as possible – playing more than a couple of defensive shots in a row will usually lose you the point. Understanding how your opponent is setting up to attack will help you neutralize more effectively.

Exploiting your opponent's grip

Understanding which grip your opponent is using when he's attacking will help you to defend more effectively because each grip favours a different type of ball speed, bounce and spin.

For more advice on exploiting your opponent's grip: see page 27 (when serving); pages 28–29 (when serving against double-handed grips); and pages 70–73 (when you are attacking from the baseline).

YOUR OPPONENT'S FOREHAND GRIP　　　　**WHAT TO LOOK FOR**

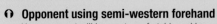

Opponent using continental forehand
Opponents using a continental grip will want to attack off a low-bouncing ball. Expect his shots to be hit very flat (without much spin) and with pace, often hitting to a good depth in the court.

Opponent using semi-western forehand
Your opponent will be most comfortable making contact around waist to chest height using this grip. It helps him to generate topspin, which will allow him to hit with angle as well as depth.

Opponent using eastern forehand
This grip will see your opponent looking to attack short balls bouncing at waist height. Although able to generate some topspin on his shots, he will use depth and pace as his strongest weapons.

Opponent using western forehand
Comfortable hitting balls at shoulder height, this player will use lots of topspin to attack with. Expect the ball to bounce high on your side, so a deeper court position might help you.

⌒ Opponent using an eastern backhand

This opponent will be most effective attacking balls between knee and waist height. He'll be able to hit with topspin and pace – particularly against short balls he can move forwards on.

⌒ Opponent using a strong eastern backhand

This grip will allow your opponent to hit with more aggressive topspin against higher bouncing balls (between waist and shoulder height). Expect the ball to bounce high on your side too, so a deeper baseline position is recommended when defending.

⌒ Opponent using a double-handed backhand 50:50

This opponent will have a variety of attacking options. He'll usually look to contact the ball inside the baseline (using the pace of your shot to attack with) and can deal with the higher-bouncing ball due to the strength of two hands on the grip.

⌒ Opponent using a double-handed backhand 25:75

The lack of involvement of the bottom hand allows the top hand to dominate on this shot. An opponent will hit quite flat with pace, and will also be able to create tricky angles off higher balls.

⌒ Opponent using a double-handed backhand 75:25

The dominant bottom hand allows an opponent to hit with more topspin than the other double-handed grips. He will also be comfortable attacking the higher-bouncing ball. Mis-timed shots are more likely to go down the line.

KEY THINGS TO CONSIDER

▶▶ **HOW HIGH?** Note how high your opponent likes to let the ball bounce when attacking from the baseline.

▶▶ **WHERE ARE THE STRINGS?** Looking closely at your opponent's racket strings will often tell you the direction of his next shot.

Reading your opponent's swing

Noting your opponent's swing shape, as well as his court position, will give you some great tactical clues as to how and where he might be planning to attack.

DEFENDING AGAINST AN AGGRESSIVE FOREHAND

Many players prefer to attack with their forehand. Using more parts of their body in a longer, more complex chain of movements produces racket-head speed that results in power and spin – harder to achieve

on the backhand side. Your court positioning is crucial when defending against this type of shot. Taking up a deeper position can allow a little extra time to prepare, although it is important to regain a more neutral position as soon as you can.

Opponents who use a smaller swing on their forehand side will try to create time pressure on you with aggressive court positioning. They will use the pace of your shots in order to send their shots back so quickly that you don't have enough time to prepare. In this case, preparing quickly for your shots is probably more important than dropping deeper.

FOREHAND ATTACK   **WHAT TO LOOK FOR**

◖ **Attacking with power**
An opponent who uses a longer, coordinated chain of movements is able to attack with more power and spin.

◖ **Attacking with accuracy**
An opponent who uses a short swing will use time pressure and accuracy to dominate you.

YOUR OPPONENT'S STANCE   **WHAT TO LOOK FOR**

◖ **Attacking with a closed stance**
An opponent who uses a closed stance on his forehand (his front foot is positioned across his back foot) will tend to attack down the line or the middle of the court more often.

◖ **Attacking with a semi-open stance**
An opponent who uses a semi-open stance has a wider range of options. You need to consider his grip, court position and previous attacking tactics.

DEFENDING AGAINST AN AGGRESSIVE BACKHAND

Opponents will attack very differently depending on whether they use a single- or a double-handed backhand. In general, the single-handed player can hit a wider variety of shots (topspin, slice, short angle, drop shot), whereas the double-hander will be able to hit the ball early, accurately and with disguise.

When a single-hander uses slice to attack, you will notice the racket head being lifted above the ball before contact is made – so be prepared for the ball to bounce low on your side of the court. Sometimes you can also read the intended direction of the slice by looking at the angle of your opponent's racket just before he makes contact with the ball.

READING DIRECTION **WHAT TO LOOK FOR**

Hitting crosscourt
This opponent is setting up to hit crosscourt. His strings are pointing across the court as he tries to hit around the outside edge of the ball. Note how his non-hitting arm is positioned close to his body to allow for more body rotation which helps the ball go crosscourt.

Hitting down the line
This opponent is shaping up to hit down the line. Note how he keeps his non-hitting arm behind him to help maintain his balance and to avoid over-rotating through the shot.

BACKHAND ATTACK **WHAT TO LOOK FOR**

Backhand with topspin
You can spot when an opponent intends to hit with a single-handed topspin backhand because the racket face will point more towards the side of the court on his backswing.

Backhands with closed stance
Both the single backhand (above left) and the double backhand (above right) have a greater chance of being hit down the line or down the middle of the court than of being hit crosscourt when using a closed stance.

Using patterns of play to defend effectively

There are certain sequences of shots that you can play when you're under pressure that will give you the best possible chance of shifting the balance of play back your way.

SINGLES

DEFENDING AGAINST AN ATTACK DOWN THE LINE
Buying time to recover is the key to defending against an attack down the line – so playing a high, deep shot either crosscourt or down the middle of the court is recommended. As long as your opponent decides to stay put on the baseline, this type of shot will give you more time to reposition yourself for your next shot. It also reduces the angle available for your opponent's next shot and is hit with the highest margin of error possible (over the lowest part of the net and into the longest part of the court).

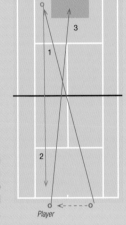

Opponent

Player

➲ **Slowing the ball down**
This player hits a backhand slice deep down the middle of the court (3). He uses slice to slow the ball down to allow that split-second of extra time to recover.

PREVENTING THE BACK BEHIND ATTACK
It is important not to anticipate the down-the-line attack illustrated in the above diagram too early – otherwise your opponent may hit back crosscourt behind you to win the point. The use of a well-timed split-step as your opponent is about to make contact with the ball will ensure that you remain balanced and ready to move in either direction. This rule applies even if you are completely out of position.

DEFENDING AGAINST THE SHORT ANGLE
The short-angle groundstroke will tend to drag you short and wide of the court. Try to move straight to the ball in this situation and do not give your opponent much angle to work with on his next shot.

Opponent

Player

➲ **Deep middle reply**
This player has moved straight to the short, wide ball (1) and has played a deep middle shot as a reply (2).

DEFENDING AGAINST THE DROP SHOT
The first rule is to get to the ball as quickly as you can. If you can play a shot back, then your options will depend on the positioning of your opponent. If you spot your opponent on the baseline, then a drop shot back is a good choice. If this is too difficult, any type of deep shot down the middle is ideal. Finally, if your opponent moves in to the net, then either a lob or a shot straight at him can work well.

☊ **Drop shot back**
Playing a drop shot back is useful against an opponent who stays on the baseline.

PRACTICE: limit defensive shots

During practice, allow yourself only two defensive shots in a row to get back to neutral – otherwise you lose the point immediately.

DOUBLES

DEALING WITH A CROSSCOURT BUILDING SHOT

Defending effectively when in a one-up/one-back formation is crucial. This formation will often happen when your baseline opponent has hit a crosscourt groundstroke that has pushed you deep and/or wide of the baseline. In this situation, your opponent at the net will be looking to intercept your reply with a winning volley.

The first thing to look for is whether your net opponent is moving across the net in anticipation too early. If you spot this, hitting down his line is an excellent choice.

You could also choose to lob down the line when under pressure from a crosscourt attacking groundstroke in order to buy time.

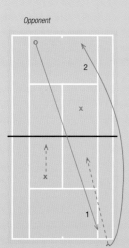

◠ Moving forwards

The lob (2) is hit over the head of the net opponent, allowing the player to move forwards.

◠ Defending a short lob

Your partner should move back quickly in order to defend a short lob (2).

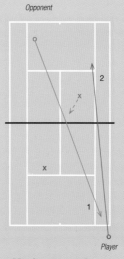

◠ Moving too early

The opponent at the net has clearly moved too early, leaving a big space down his line to hit into (2).

◠ Defending against the lob down the line

When your partner at the net has been lobbed down the line by your opponent on the baseline (1), it is important that you both coordinate a defence quickly. The best way is to switch sides with your partner. This means you move across the baseline to play a groundstroke down the line (2), while your partner moves across the net so that he is opposite the net opponent.

TIP: getting a heads-up

If you know your partner is planning to hit a lob, angle your body position slightly so that you can track the flight path of the ball from his racket more easily. This will allow you to respond quicker after your partner's shot.

3 TRADING FROM THE BASELINE

'Trading' refers to moments in a rally when neither player (or team, in doubles) holds an advantage. The ability to trade is vital when playing tennis – it gives you a chance to learn about the strengths and weaknesses of your opponent, as well as position yourself ideally for your next attack.

TRADING AT THE START Trading well at the start of a match is particularly important. You don't usually know what your opponent is thinking or feeling about the match, so starting consistently and playing within your capability is a smart move.

PRACTICE: alternative scoring

Play practice points with a weighted scoring system in order to encourage consistent trading skills from the baseline. An unforced error from your opponent is worth 3 points, a forced error is worth 2 points and a winning shot is worth 1 point.

AVOIDING AN OPPONENT'S STRENGTH This trading tactic is employed when you need to avoid an opponent's strength from the baseline. Typically, this means hitting consistently and accurately to your opponent's other side, or hitting a specific type of shot that restricts his strength. For example, when you're facing an opponent with a strong forehand, trading wide to his forehand opens up his backhand side for your next shot.

USING THE TRADING SWITCH Simply changing the direction of the ball when in a trading baseline rally will challenge your opponent – particularly one who doesn't move efficiently. This involves hitting crosscourt and down the line without adding any extra pace, spin or accuracy to your shot. You will be amazed at how many attacking opportunities are created when you do this well enough.

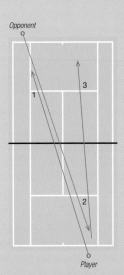

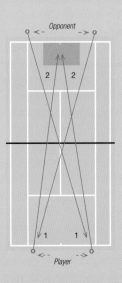

Playing pattern: avoiding the forehand

This player avoids his opponent's forehand by hitting wide to it once (1), before quickly switching to playing to his backhand side (3).

Playing pattern: trading down the middle

If your opponent's forehand and backhand are equally strong, trade down the middle of the court to reduce the angle and space available (2).

⌕ Attacking opportunity

This player hits a trading backhand slice down the line but his opponent anticipates a crosscourt shot instead. This creates an attacking opportunity almost effortlessly.

TRADING WITH THE JUNK BALL A fun trading tactic that can really frustrate an opponent is to play from the baseline, constantly mixing up the pace, spin and depth of your shots. This is particularly effective against an opponent who likes to find a consistent groove. You will throw him off his rhythm and timing, and may even get inside his head.

SLOW BALL TRADING Many opponents like a ball that is hit with consistent pace. This is particularly true of double-handers and counter-attackers who play from on or around the baseline. In this situation, slowing the pace of your shots when trading can frustrate them and reduce their attacking opportunities.

TRADING WITH THE SLICE BALL A ball hit with slice is a great trading shot – it maintains your position in the rally because it is so difficult to attack against. It is very useful against opponents with extreme grips (the low bounce will prevent them from attacking effectively), and it travels slightly slower through the air – giving you a bit more time to decide on your next move.

KEY THINGS TO CONSIDER

HOW NERVOUS ARE THEY? Can you sense how nervous your opponent is feeling?

WHAT DO THEY WANT? Look out for the shot your opponent likes best and try to avoid it on the big points.

PICK AND MIX How can you mix up your play to frustrate your opponent the most?

➲ **Trade with slice**
Use a slice backhand to mix up the pace of your shots and so frustrate your opponent.

TIP: space not pace

Play the space-not-pace game to develop a better feel for the ball. Play practice points where neither player is allowed to hit with any pace – points can only be won by accuracy and variety. This is a great game for improving your court awareness and control of the ball.

net play

Playing at the net is one of the most exciting aspects of tennis – rallies are often fast and dynamic, and can change the momentum of a match instantly. Although preparation time is shorter than when playing at the baseline, experienced players will look out for visual clues to anticipate their opponent's next shot. This chapter shows you how to spot these clues and explains the type of approach shots you can use to limit your opponent's passing shot options. It also suggests how to maintain a positive net position in singles and doubles, even if you are under pressure.

1 Approaching the net in singles

Learn about the types of approach shot you can use, with an emphasis on those shots that will most limit your opponent's options.

See pages 90–95

2 Approaching the net in doubles

Discover the various patterns of play that your team can adopt based on your court position, as well as on what your opponents are planning to do.

See pages 96–101

3 Winning at the net when under pressure

Look at what you can do if your opponent has gained the upper hand in a rally when playing both singles and doubles matches.

See pages 102–103

APPROACHING THE NET
IN SINGLES

There are two ways to approach the net: the planned approach and the instinctive approach. A planned approach is when you decide before you hit the ball that you will follow your shot into the net. An instinctive approach is when you decide after you've hit a shot from the baseline that you are going to approach the net. Both tactics can be effective, but each requires a completely different set of skills.

Singles playing patterns: using the planned approach

The planned approach is the more traditional way of approaching the net. You need to plan your approach in advance and then work out where your opponent is most likely to play once you are at the net.

You can plan to approach the net even before the start of the point. For instance, you may plan to serve and then move forwards to volley; approach the net after a second serve return; or approach with a backhand slice groundstroke on the first incoming ball that lands inside the service line. You'll have decided on these strategies before a ball has been struck. Or, you may decide within the point that your next shot will be an approach – the approach is still planned, but you've made the decision over a shorter timeline.

APPROACHING DOWN THE LINE One of the most popular ways to move forwards to the net from the baseline, the planned approach down the line limits your opponent's options and allows you to cover the most important areas of the court. The only area that you'll leave open is the acute crosscourt passing shot, which is extremely difficult for your opponent to hit when under pressure. With this in mind, follow the line of the ball into the net rather than automatically covering the centre of the net.

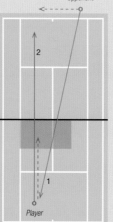

➲ Down the line, then follow the ball
The player approaches the net after hitting a backhand groundstroke down the line (2). She then follows the line of the ball, which means covering the left and centre of the court, and leaving the far right area open.

KEY THINGS TO CONSIDER

▶ **PLAN YOUR ATTACK** Make plans in advance based on your strengths and your opponent's weaknesses. Look out for the size of your opponent's swing, the grip she is using and where she is positioned on the baseline.

▶ **BE SNEAKY** Approach the net instinctively when you sense your opponent is under pressure. An open racket face may indicate a more 'floated' defensive shot from your opponent.

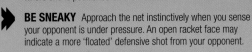

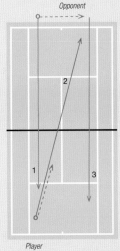

APPROACHING CROSSCOURT
Approach crosscourt with more caution than when approaching down the line as this movement creates more of a space for your opponent to hit into if she is not put under enough pressure.

➲ **Deep crosscourt approach**
The player has not put her opponent under enough pressure (2) and so is punished by a winning down-the-line passing shot (3).

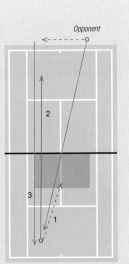

∩ Down the line, then move to centre
The same backhand groundstroke approach shot is hit down the line (2), but this time the player automatically moves to the centre of the net instead of following the ball. This leaves her left line too exposed. If under pressure, a down-the-line ball (3) may be the best shot option for her opponent.

∩ Short and wide
➲ **crosscourt approach**
This opponent is pressurized by the short, wide approach (2), which allows the player to close in on the net and play a volley winner into the open court (4). The short-angle crosscourt approach is often more effective than the deep crosscourt approach as it drags your opponent up the court as well as across it. Players with single-handed slice backhands hit this shot particularly well.

In the photograph above, the player is closing in after putting her opponent under pressure with the short angle of her approach shot.

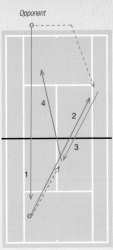

APPROACHING DOWN THE MIDDLE You can restrict your opponent's passing shot options, and leave her no obvious space or angle to work with, by approaching down the middle of the court. Experienced players often hit here when they have been forced into the net by a short ball, or when they want to approach against an opponent who prefers the ball to be hit wide (a counter-attacker or a tall player, for example). The approach down the middle is also used as a surprise tactic when a player senses that her opponent is feeling nervous and wants to hurry her into hitting a passing shot.

Just as for a down-the-line approach (see page 90), following the line of your approach shot is good advice. This means covering the centre of the court while giving up the two wide spaces to the side of you, which are very difficult to hit from your opponent's central position.

If you spot your opponent standing very deep behind the baseline, then the short, middle approach shot is a good option. This is different from a drop shot (see page 59) because is not hit quite as short.

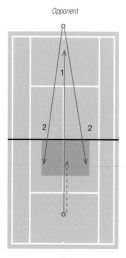

Opponent

Player

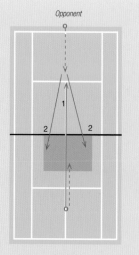

Opponent

Player

◯ Deep approach down the middle

A deep approach shot down the middle of the court (1) severely restricts what your opponent can do with her passing shot (2). The only space on the court is extremely wide of centre and behind you. As a result, it is important to be ready to cover a lob in this situation.

◯ STAGE 1: Player moves forwards after short approach

This player is approaching down the middle of the court with a short, slice backhand. The bounce of the ball will stay low, making it very difficult for her opponent to hit an effective passing shot.

◯ STAGE 2: Player then positions herself close to net

Note how this player has closed in on the net in anticipation of a weak reply from her opponent.

◯ Short approach
↻ down the middle

An advantage of using the short, middle approach instead of the deep, middle approach is that it usually prevents your opponent hitting a lob. This is because there is far less space to hit into behind you from such a short position on the court. Note how the short, middle approach (1) reduces the space to the side and over the top of the player.

OTHER PLANNED APPROACH
SHOTS Take a close look at your opponent's grip, swing shape and court position to highlight other ways of approaching the net. For example, opponents who use a continental or eastern forehand grip won't like playing against a higher-bouncing ball (they will prefer to make contact with the ball from a lower position). Therefore, a loop hit high over the net with topspin may work well.

⟳ High ball approach shot
Not only does the high bounce of this ball challenge the opponent, but it also gives the player plenty of time to close in on the net.

⋒ Fast-paced approach
An opponent who uses big swings on her groundstrokes will be challenged by a fast-paced approach shot since it cuts down her swing time severely. Bear in mind that the faster you hit your approach, the faster it will be hit back to you! This means that you may not have time to close in on the net fully.

PRACTICE: last shot first
A great exercise to help you develop winning net patterns is to work on the last shot of the rally first. Practise the way you ideally want to finish your points at the net (smash, drive volley or volley) and then work backwards to the beginning of the point. What shot would you need to hit before your winning volley? What type of serve or return would you hit to create this opportunity?

⋒ Short and low approach shot
This opponent is struggling to reach a short, low approach and is likely to hit the ball back short and high as a result.

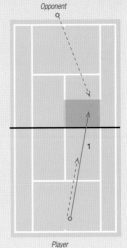

⊃ Closing in
Reduce your opponent's options by closing in on the net after hitting a short and low approach (1).

Singles playing patterns: using the instinctive approach

When using the instinctive approach, you'll need to decide to move forwards to the net after you have hit your groundstroke. You may sense that your opponent is under pressure and quickly move forwards to volley or smash her next shot. This so-called 'sneak' tactic requires good anticipation skills, as well as an understanding of what your opponent's most likely next shot will be.

Experienced players often 'ghost' into the net as soon as they have read their opponent's court position (tactical anticipation, see page 14) and shot preparation (technical anticipation, see page 15). If they know for sure that their opponent will struggle, then they often won't wait to see the ball being hit – they'll be on the approach already.

WHAT TO LOOK FOR

SNEAKING TO THE BACKHAND SIDE

This sneak tactic is a popular move – especially against the double-hander who is forced to take one hand off her grip to play the ball back. If she has been forced to do this, then you can almost guarantee that her reply will be weak.

↺ **Your opponent's court position**

Look at where your opponent is playing her next shot from. This will indicate whether you can approach the net before you hit your next shot. Note how deep and wide this opponent's court position is, as well as the physical pressure she is under with the lunge she is making.

↷ **Angle of opponent's racket face**

Try to spot the angle of your opponent's racket face as she prepares to hit the ball. An open racket face usually means that a higher, slower ball will be played back, which may be perfect to volley.

↻ **Spot ball characteristics**

As your opponent hits her shot, try to spot whether the ball is slow and high enough to volley. If you respond quickly, you may still have time to hit the ball out of the air.

SNEAKING TO THE FOREHAND SIDE

Approaching by hitting to the forehand side is also an effective tactic as long as you put your opponent under enough pressure. Remember that many opponents favour this side and most will have a wider reach to defend with.

Choose your volley

The sneak volley: The opponent is usually defending deep behind the baseline, so players often hit a short angle volley when approaching the net. This forces the opponent into covering the maximum amount of court in a short time.

The drive volley: The longer it takes you to decide to approach, the less ground you will cover moving forwards. In this situation, a drive volley (a volley hit with a longer swing, similar to a groundstroke) may be your best option.

WHAT TO LOOK FOR

Your opponent's court position

The depth and width of your opponent's court position will strongly influence how well she can defend. This opponent is too deep and wide to be able to defend with any force. In this situation it would be wise to sneak into the net as quickly as possible.

PRACTICE: sneaks for bonuses

Award bonus points for recognizing a sneak opportunity – even if the point is lost. Winning with a sneak approach will win you 2 points; losing with a sneak approach will prevent your opponent from scoring (you both win 1 point).

Angle of opponent's racket face

Most forehands are hit with some form of topspin, so an opponent hitting with an open racket face will potentially mean a defensive shot is being played. This could prove an easy ball to volley against.

Spot ball characteristics

Spotting the height, speed and direction of your opponent's defensive shot will indicate whether you should move forwards. If your opponent is under extreme pressure, moving forwards is a smart move even if you don't manage to volley the ball. This is because the incoming ball is likely to land short, so an early aggressive groundstroke may be just as effective as a volley.

APPROACHING THE NET
IN DOUBLES

Strong net play is crucial in doubles since the lack of space on the court means that most points are won and lost at the net. For this reason, most key doubles tactics are based around taking control of the net.

Doubles playing patterns: using the planned approach

The planned approach in doubles is probably the most commonly used tactic in tennis. On a doubles court both teams start in a one-up/one-back formation, which is tailor-made for one team to take command of the net. You should aim to move shoulder-to-shoulder with your partner, which means moving forwards, backwards and sideways as a unit. This parallel play prevents any major gaps from appearing between you.

USING THE PLANNED SERVE AND VOLLEY In order to approach the net, a player serves and then follows in to join her net partner – usually on the first serve, but sometimes on the second serve. Topspin on the second serve will make the ball kick up after the bounce, allowing a split-second longer for positioning. If you spot the returning opponent standing too centrally on the baseline, then serving out wide and following in to the net is a powerful option. Or, serve-and-volleying down the middle of the court is a favourite choice as it reduces the angle available to the returner. This lack of angle means that you and your partner can maintain a close formation at the net with a good chance of commanding the centre of the court. This positioning forces your opponents into having to hit through or over you.

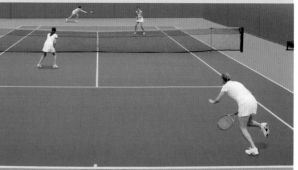

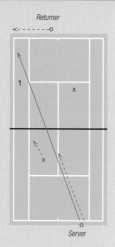

↻ Moving as one
This server and her partner move as a team towards where the ball is served, preventing any big gaps from appearing between them.

➲ Serve out wide from the deuce court
The serve has been hit out wide from the deuce court. The server then follows the line of her serve, which means positioning herself more towards the left-hand side of the net.

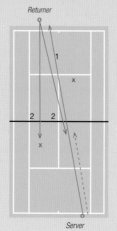

↻ Serve down the middle
↻ from the deuce court
The serve has been hit down the middle from the deuce court (1). The server then moves forwards and forms a very central net position with her partner; the most likely return will be somewhere down the middle of the court (2).

The photograph above shows how the middle serve allows a doubles team to successfuly maintain control over the centre of the court.

USING THE CHIP AND CHARGE This tactic sees the returner hit a return crosscourt and then immediately join her partner at the net. It is usually planned in advance and will often prove successful against a weak second serve. The chip and charge is an effective tactic to use against opponents keen to approach the net themselves, who don't like being rushed, or who have a particularly weak groundstroke side. Hit the return with either topspin or slice – depending on what will be most challenging for your opponents.

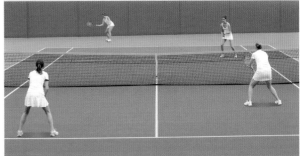

KEY THINGS TO CONSIDER

▶ **RUB SHOULDERS** Note how well aligned you are with your partner when you are both at the net.

▶ **USE SOME SET PLAYS** Try to plan a combination of your best shots to approach the net with.

▶ **JOIN YOUR PARTNER** Look out for your opponent's angle of racket face, the amount of pressure she is under and the type of ball coming towards you to see if you can sneak in to the net to join your partner.

STAGE 1: Player uses a blocked return
This player uses a blocked return, which will travel slightly slower through the air and give her time to approach the net.

STAGE 2: Player joins partner at net
The returner then follows the line of her return to join her partner at the net.

DOUBLES FORMATIONS

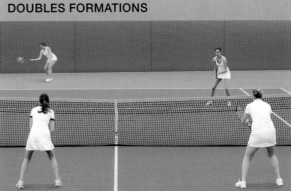

Players aligned shoulder to shoulder
Moving together as a team when approaching and playing at the net is crucial.

Players positioned too far apart
These players are positioned too far away from each other and at a diagonal.

USING THE GROUNDSTROKE APPROACH Just as in singles, there will be times when the serve and return do not create an opportunity for both players in a team to approach the net. In this situation, a crosscourt baseline rally develops between the server and returner. Either player now has a chance to approach the net behind a crosscourt groundstroke.

Approaching crosscourt is safer in doubles than in singles because there is no space down the line for your opponent to hit into (your partner is standing at the net covering this possibility). Therefore, you can use a variety of approaches based on what you see at the other end of the court.

DEEP CROSSCOURT

Hitting deep crosscourt always gives you a chance to approach and play from the net. The depth of your shot allows you extra time to close in on the net and prevents your opponent from being too aggressive.

Opt for a higher shot with spin against an opponent who uses a flatter grip such as a continental or an eastern forehand grip or, alternatively, a deep, but lower-bouncing, approach against an opponent who uses a more extreme grip such as a western forehand or strong eastern backhand grip. For both shots, try to hit your approach away from the opponent at the net — so preventing her from intercepting with a volley.

SHORT CROSSCOURT

If you spot your baseline opponent standing too deep, or if she is using an extreme grip, then hitting short and low crosscourt is another excellent way of approaching the net. If hit well enough, there is a good chance that your opponent's reply will be high and slow, making it easier to hit away a volley or smash winner.

♭ High, looped
♮ approach shot

Hit a high, looped approach shot crosscourt to give you time to move forwards and join your partner at the net (1). Your opponent will struggle to deal with the depth and bounce of your shot (2).

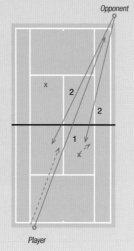

Opponent

Player

♭ Low, wide approach
♮ shot with slice

Hit a backhand slice low and wide (1), forcing your opponent into scraping the ball back (2) in reply. You and your partner can then move in close to the net to finish off with a volley or smash.

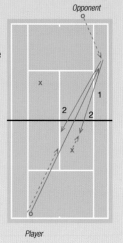

Opponent

Player

USING THE LOB DOWN THE LINE An excellent approach method, the lob down the line can be used as a return or in a crosscourt baseline rally. It can cause confusion within an opposing team as both opponents will need to switch positions. It is best used if your opponent is standing too close to the net, if you know she has a weak smash, or simply as a way of changing a match's momentum.

If you use the lob to return serve, then let your partner know in advance so that she can position herself. If you hit a great lob, she'll be looking to move forwards straight away; if you hit a poor lob, she will automatically try to retreat to defend the inevitable smash.

For more on doubles net play, see pages 100–101 and page 103.

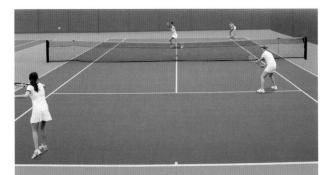

⊙ STAGE 1: Player uses a lifted lob
This player returns with a lifted lob down the line before moving forwards to join her partner at the net.

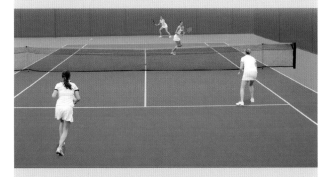

⊙ STAGE 2: Player then moves in to net
As the player moves in to the net, both opponents have to switch court positions.

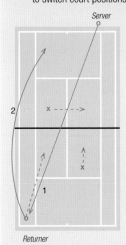

Server

2

Returner

↻ Lob and follow-up
Hit a backhand lob down the line over the head of your opponent at the net (2) before moving swiftly forwards as your opponents are forced into switching positions.

⊙ Net partner moves forwards after a successful lob
Your partner should move forwards if the lob is successful. The better the lob, the more chance of a higher, defensive return being played back.

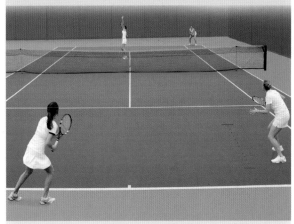

⊙ Net partner moves backwards to defend against a smash
Your partner must watch her opposing net partner carefully. If it looks as if the lob is going to be smashed, she may have time to move back slightly more.

Doubles playing patterns: using the instinctive approach

There will be times in doubles when you or your partner will instinctively look to approach the net to volley or smash. Again, this will depend very much on your opponents' court position before and after you hit your shot.

WHEN SERVING A strong serve will often create opportunities for either you or your partner at the net to play a volley – even without planning to. If a defensive return gets past your partner at the net (perhaps because it is too wide for her), it is up to you to decide whether to move forwards or stay on the baseline. The more quickly you make this decision, the better.

Things to look out for are the angle of your opponent's racket when returning, the amount of pressure she is under and the type of ball coming back towards you. For example, if the ball is high and slow, then hitting a drive volley can be a great shot. Players often find that they end up playing a volley from around the service line if they have instinctively moved forwards after spotting a weak return (i.e. they run out of time to move further forwards). Playing a drive volley with more pace and spin is exactly what is needed to maintain pressure on their opponents from this position.

➲ Drive volley
↻ The server sneaks forwards to play a drive volley (3) because the return floated past her partner at the net (2). The server then plays straight at her net opponent who is now under extreme pressure due to the pace and spin of the ball.

In the photograph below, the server is playing a drive volley at her net opponent.

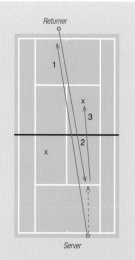

WHEN RETURNING

There will be occasions when your return sets up an opportunity to approach the net (just as it does when you are serving). This can occur on second serve returns in particular as you look to pressurize your opponents with pace and accuracy. Experienced players often sneak in instinctively after hitting a dominant wide return – this allows them to split their opponents with a follow-up volley down the middle of the court.

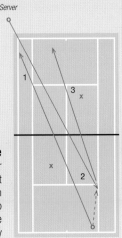

Server

∩ Volley down the middle
➲ The return (1) forces the server into playing a defensive shot from a deep and wide position (2). This allows the returner to move forwards and play a simple volley down the middle away from both opponents (3).

Returner

WHEN PLAYING FROM THE BASELINE

Trading well with deep and accurate groundstrokes crosscourt will create opportunities for you to approach and play from the net. Successful doubles teams usually develop an understanding, which means that either player has a licence to intercept a groundstroke to volley a ball they can dominate with – whether planned or not.

Ways to approach instinctively include hitting deep and wide, hitting short and low or hitting a drop shot. All these shots can potentially pressurize your baseline opponent into defending to the point where you can follow in and volley, or your partner can intercept with a volley.

∩ STAGE 1: Player hits a drop shot
This player hits a forehand drop shot and senses that her baseline opponent is really struggling to reach the ball.

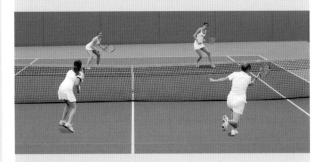

∩ STAGE 2: Player then uses a sneak volley
The player instinctively moves forwards to the net to play a sneak volley down to the feet of the opposing net player.

Opponent

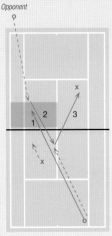

➲ Drop shot, then sneak volley
The player spots her opponent standing deep behind the baseline and so hits a drop shot (1). Sensing that her opponent is struggling to reach the ball, she then instinctively moves in and volleys the reply straight at the opponent at the net (3).

Player

There will be times in singles and doubles when you are under pressure at the net, perhaps because you have been lured in by your opponent or just haven't hit a very good approach shot. Either way, you need to develop some kind of survival strategy.

Singles: holding your ground

When you find yourself a sitting target at the net, stay calm and hold your ground. Less experienced players often move to cover one side, guessing which way the passing shot will be hit far too early. This simply helps your opponent make a decision to hit to the other side. Your best strategy is to maintain a central court position and stay there because this forces your opponent into deciding where to hit. Your opponent may also be expecting you to move and may get unnerved when you don't.

You can also try playing down the middle of the court when under pressure from a passing shot or lob. Reducing the angle and space available to your opponent must be your first priority.

KEY THINGS TO CONSIDER

▶ **DON'T PANIC** Don't guess where you think your opponent will hit a passing shot – if you don't know, hold your ground.

▶ **MIDDLE IS SAFEST** Choose your shot at the net based on the amount of pressure you are under. Remember that the middle of the court is a great option if you need to defend.

▶ **SPLIT WHEN IN COMMAND** In doubles, look for a chance to play wide when in command of the point so that you create bigger spaces on the court to hit into.

◑ **Hold your ground**
This player is holding a central court position, which forces her opponent into making a decision on which direction to hit her shot.

◑ **Don't move too early**
This player has hit the panic button too early and so allowed her opponent a free shot into the space that has been created.

TIP: use the double bluff
A good strategy is to fake a move to one side – then move back to cover the other side. It's crucial to fake your movement early enough so that you can regain your balance in time to cover the other side once the passing shot has been played. You'll often find that you have lured your opponent into hitting to the side that you are actually covering.

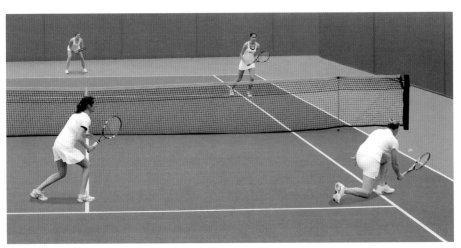

 Maintaining a strong unit

The volleyer's partner moves across the court with her, maintaining a strong central unit. The volley is played deep, down the middle of the court (1), thus reducing the angle and space available for the opponent's next shot.

Opponent

Player

Doubles: defending as a team

You will need to defend your position at the net even more often in doubles than in singles. Your goal is to maintain command over the centre of the net as much as possible. This means that you and your partner must stay close together and stand your ground as a unit, forcing your opponents into hitting to the sides of the court or over the top of you.

When one of you is forced to volley from a wide position, the other player must move across the court to fill any gaps down the middle. The same principle applies when one of you is lobbed. Hitting the defensive smash back down the middle of the court is your best option because it allows you to stay close together and reduces the space on the court. If you are both at the net and the lob goes over your head, then your partner needs to quickly drop back to the baseline to retrieve the ball while you switch your net position to the other side.

DOUBLES: SUCCESSFUL PATTERNS OF PLAY AT THE NET

Opponent	*Opponent*	*Opponent*
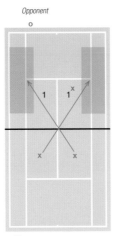		
Player	*Player*	*Player*

Central smash area
This is the target area to play the volley and smash into when you are under pressure at the net as a team (1).

Splitting opponents
When you are in a more dominant position you can afford to hit wide of the court, splitting your opponents with the angle of your shots (1).

Switch to retrieve a lob
The player who has been lobbed (1) switches net positions while her partner drops back to retrieve the lob (2). The same switch could happen in a one-up/one-back formation with the baseline player moving across to retrieve the lob.

your opponent's net play

Less experienced players often feel pressurized when an opponent approaches the net, so this chapter shows how to spot an approach shot even before it has been hit and then how to counter it from the baseline. It also explains how you can tempt your opponents into hitting to a certain area by combining smart court positioning with a reading of their favourite playing patterns in both singles and doubles.

1 Limiting your opponent's options

Learn about the various approach shots that your opponent may use and how you can counter them most effectively.

See pages 106–113

2 Bringing opponents into the net to attack

Find out the best ways to deliberately bring your opponent into the net in order to attack past, through or over them.

See pages 114–119

1 LIMITING YOUR OPPONENT'S OPTIONS AT THE NET

An opponent or opposing team may approach and play from the net in a number of different ways. It is important to know what options are available to you based on each type of approach. The two key areas to look at are where your opponent hits to and where he positions himself at the net.

First, note the direction of the ball as it comes towards you to determine the angle available for your passing shot or lob. The position your opponent takes up once at the net should also give you a strong clue as to your best option – less experienced opponents will often leave themselves exposed at the net.

You also need to work out how effective your previous shot has been, as this will ultimately determine whether an approach is imminent. Prior experience may tell you, for example, that your ball landed too short, or was hit too softly – meaning that you should be ready for your opponent to attack.

Singles playing patterns: defending with the two-ball pass

Remember, just because your opponent has approached the net doesn't mean that you have to hit a winner straight away. The two-ball pass tactic is recommended in some cases because it helps you stay calm under pressure and can turn a defensive situation into a winning one. This tactic requires you to hit a high-percentage passing shot straight at your opponent, low to the feet or hard, with the deliberate intention of making him play a challenging volley. This will often open up the court for you to hit a winning pass or lob as your second shot instead of your first.

In general, an approach shot can be hit in one of three directions: down the line, crosscourt or down the middle of the court. Each one presents a different set of shot options depending on how much pressure you are under.

KEY THINGS TO CONSIDER

 THE ANGLE IS KEY Note the angle of your opponent's approach shot since this will often determine what options you have for your passing shot or lob.

 LOOK FOR THE SPACE Sometimes your opponent will leave a space at the net for you to hit into without realizing.

 DOUBLE TROUBLE Using a two-ball passing shot combination can be far more effective than trying to hit a winner straight away.

🎧 **Opponent approaching the net**
Always try to make your opponent play one more shot – no matter how much pressure you are put under from his approach.

🎧 **Opponent playing at the net**
Playing straight at this opponent when he is at the net may create a chance to pass him with your next shot.

PLAYING AGAINST THE LINE APPROACH Looking carefully at the angle of your opponent's racket face may give away in which direction his approach will be hit — especially on his backhand side.

PLAYING AGAINST THE CROSSCOURT APPROACH The angle of your opponent's racket face will look slightly different when he approaches crosscourt. He will need to hit more around the outside edge of the ball.

➲ **Responding to a line approach**

The opponent approaches the net down the line (1). You could hit a crosscourt passing shot (2) over the lowest part of the net and into the longest part of the court. Using this as the first shot in a two-ball pass tactic may create a chance to hit a winning pass with your next shot.

Alternatively, a deep lob hit crosscourt (3) could also prove effective — especially against an opponent who is very close to the net. (A lob down the line is also an option — particularly if played against a right-hander over his backhand side.)

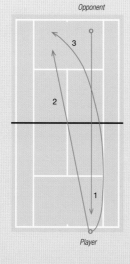

➲ **Responding to a crosscourt approach**

Here, the opponent approaches crosscourt (1). Your best reply depends on how much pressure you have been put under. If possible, a passing shot hit down the line (2) is a good option because the ball is hit away from your approaching opponent. However, if you are under a lot of pressure through the depth or power of the approach, then the lob crosscourt (3) or the down-the-middle reply (4) may prove more effective because they both carry a higher margin for error.

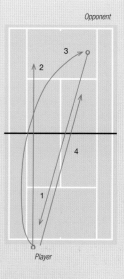

WHAT TO LOOK FOR

♩ **Opponent approaching down the line with slice**
This opponent's racket face is pointing straight down the line, indicating that the ball will be hit in this direction. The racket head is above the height of the ball which, along with this grip, shows the approach will be hit with slice. Expect a lower-bouncing ball.

♩ **Opponent using crosscourt approach**
Your opponent's racket will point across the court rather than straight down it prior to a crosscourt approach. This will be most noticeable on the backhand slice.

PLAYING AGAINST THE DEEP MIDDLE APPROACH

There are fewer angles for either you or your opponent to work with when an approach is made down the middle of the court. Do watch out, though, for an opponent who runs around his backhand in order to hit a forehand from the middle of the court. This inside-out forehand can create an angle by your opponent hitting from the inside to the outside of the ball.

PLAYING AGAINST THE SHORT APPROACH (MIDDLE AND WIDE)
Defending against a short approach shot can be tricky if you are forced to cover a lot of ground. To be most effective move straight to the ball and then reduce the space available for your opponent's next shot.

If the approach is short and wide, pushing the ball down the line forces your opponent to create an angle crosscourt to hit past you. If you are under real pressure, playing straight at your opponent is another good option.

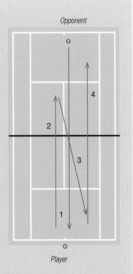

◑ Responding to a middle approach

Here, the opponent hits an approach shot deep down the middle of the court (1). This presents no obvious space for you to hit into, so using the two-ball pass tactic is your best option. Hit the passing shot straight back down the middle of the court (2) directly at your opponent, with a view to hitting your following shot as a winner (4).

You should use this tactic early on in a match in order to test the volleying ability of your opponent. Many opponents won't like the pressure of having to play consistently accurate first volleys (3) and may start forcing the volley and making mistakes as a result.

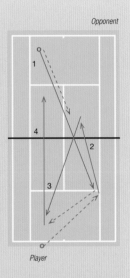

◑ Responding to a short approach

Try to move straight to the short, wide approach shot (1) and push your passing shot down the line (2). Your opponent may reply with a volley crosscourt (3), which can allow you to run across to hit a winning passing shot into the space (4).

⌒ Opponent using middle approach

This opponent is approaching down the middle of the court. The key here is not to panic and to play back down the middle of the court if necessary.

WHAT TO LOOK FOR

⌒ Opponent using short backswing

You can sometimes tell that your opponent's approach won't be hit very deep by the shorter length of his backswing.

Singles: spotting your opponent's net position

Your opponent's position at the net will influence the decision you make when hitting your passing shot or lob. Try to notice whether the space lies more behind your opponent (when he is positioned very close to the net) or whether there is more space to the side and in front of him (when he is positioned further back).

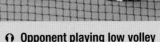

Opponent playing low volley
When your opponent is forced into playing a low volley, expect a high and possibly short ball back. Look to move forwards into the court so that you are ready to punish any weak reply.

Opponent close to net
When your opponent moves very close to the net (X), consider a lob (1) since there is a lot of space for you to hit into behind him. Alternatively, use a down-the-line passing shot (2) – your opponent will have very little time to react to this shot.

Opponent close to baseline
With a lot of space between the net and your opponent (X), hit a passing shot low, down to his feet if possible (1). This forces him to hit the volley upwards (2). Not only is this a difficult shot for your opponent to return, it also give you time to move into position for your second passing shot (3).

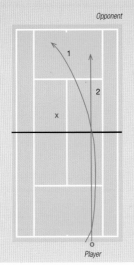

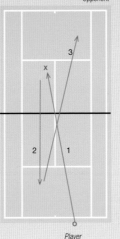

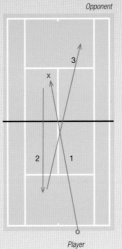

Opponent playing high volley/smash
If you see your opponent playing from high above the net (to hit a volley, drive volley or smash), move back to give yourself more space and time to defend.

TIP: test your opponent's volleys

Test your opponent's volleys early on in a match. He may be feeling nervous and lack confidence in his volleys. In fact, he may not even want to be at the net at all.

Doubles playing patterns:
defending against the serve-and-volley

There are lots of ways to neutralize an opposing team at the net and turn the situation around in your favour. In fact, taking the net away from your opponents is a key tactic when playing doubles.

One of the most popular tactics is to serve and follow in with a volley. The way in which you counter this playing tactic depends very much on the type of serve you receive, as well as on how your opponents are positioned.

DEFENDING AGAINST THE WIDE SERVE AND APPROACH If your opponents serve wide before approaching the net, then there are a number of possible responses open to you: either hitting or lobbing down the line or returning crosscourt.

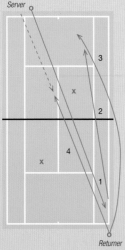

Respond to a wide serve with a down-the-line response
This player hits down the line because his opponent at the net has left a big gap for him to hit into.

Wide serve and approach
Following a wide serve (1) hit a down-the-line return (2) (see photograph, above right) if you see the server's partner positioned too far over towards the middle of the court. Or, hit a lob down the line if you're pushed very wide and deep (3). This buys you maximum time to recover your position and possibly make an approach yourself.

Alternatively, return low crosscourt and force your serving opponent into hitting a high, defensive volley that your net partner can attack (4). This shot might be a blocked return (for maximum control and timing against a strong serve) or a topspin return that dips down to your opponent's feet with spin (see photograph, right).

Respond to a wide serve with a low crosscourt response
This player chooses to pressurize the server into hitting a low volley by blocking a low, crosscourt return.

DEFENDING AGAINST THE MIDDLE SERVE
AND APPROACH If the serve is hit down the middle of the court and the server follows into the net, then you also have several options to choose from.

⮑ Middle serve and approach

The serve is hit down the middle of the court (1) and the server follows into the net. Your best options include hitting the return straight back down the middle – trying to make the server play the first volley rather than allowing his partner to intercept with his volley (2). This option keeps the court narrow and doesn't allow the opposing team to spread you wide of the court. You could also hit a lob over the server's partner at the net (3). This can be extremely effective, if hit well enough, and will force at least one of your opponents to retreat back to the baseline to play the lob back.

Yet another option is to hit low crosscourt to the incoming server to force him to defend with a low volley. Remember, this is a more precise shot, so you need to be in control of the return.

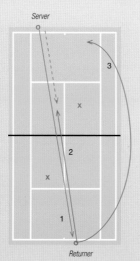

⌒ Reduce space
Playing straight back down the middle of the court reduces the space and angle available to your opponents.

USING THE BALL 4 INTERCEPT As discussed on page 63, chipping down to the feet of an incoming server is a great way of turning defence into attack. You could plan to do this before the point starts, with your partner intercepting the server's first volley with a volley of his own.

Intercepting the serving opponent's first volley requires two things. First, your return must force the server into hitting a slower, higher volley. Second, your partner at the net must time his movement across the net perfectly. This means neither moving too early (the server will volley down his line instead), nor too late (so he can't reach the server's crosscourt volley).

Planning this tactic for the fourth ball of the rally shows courage and confidence and, even if the point is lost, you will plant an important seed of doubt in your opponents' mind about what you might do next.

⮑ Volley winner

The serve is hit down the middle from the deuce court (1) and the return is chipped down to the feet of the incoming server (2). The server plays his first volley back crosscourt (3) and the returner's partner moves across to hit this volley back between the opponents as a volley winner (4).

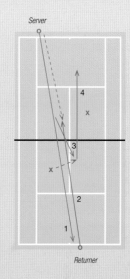

⌒ Intercept the ball
The return has been hit back to the incoming server and the returner's partner is about to intercept the server's crosscourt volley.

Doubles playing patterns: other defensive tactics

The both-back formation is a good option to use when facing an opposing team who are very dominant at the net. You and your partner should position yourselves on the baseline ready to hit through, past or over your opponents. This tactic is particularly useful for doubles teams who rely on strong groundstrokes and is also effective on slower-bouncing courts where it is relatively difficult to put the volley away for a winner.

Taking away the net target from your opponents is the key to this formation's success. Often your opponents won't know where to volley, especially when they see both of you ready to chase every ball down.

There will often be situations where both opponents are positioned at the net. Where and how you play against this formation depends very much on the amount of pressure you are under.

When you are under pressure, the golden rule is to try to reduce the space available to your opponents as much as possible. This means hitting down the middle of the court or crosscourt (including the lob), more than down the line. If you hit to the same side of the court there is a chance that your opponent may create an angle from this.

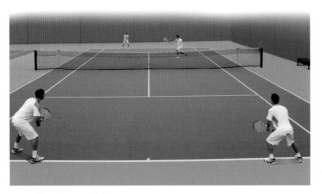

⌒ Using the both-back
⮌ formation
There is no longer a net target to aim for when you and your partner are both positioned on the baseline.

In the photograph above, the intercept volley is about to be played but there is no obvious target to hit to. Both baseline players are ready to chase any type of volley down.

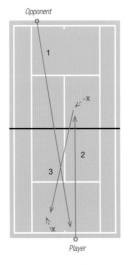

Opponent

Player

⌒ Hitting crosscourt when
⮌ under pressure
Hitting to the other side of the court when under pressure reduces the ability of your opponents to create angles on the next shot. The lob crosscourt (1) is far more effective in this situation than the drive down the line (2), which exposes you to your opponent's crosscourt volley (3).

In the photograph above, the player chooses to lob crosscourt behind the opposing team rather than down the line because this is where the biggest space is.

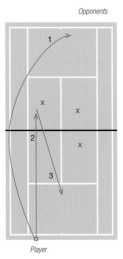

Opponents

Player

WHEN DOMINATING Your options are different when you are in a relatively dominant position against opponents at the net. In this situation you can afford to hit more down the line, which may create more space for you to hit into for your following shot. If you are inside the baseline, hitting past or through your opponents is preferable to hitting over them (there is less space available behind them the further inside the court you move).

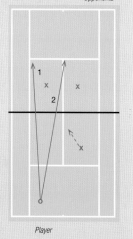

Opponents

➲ **Hitting wide**
Hit either down the line (1) or down the middle (2) of the court when you are in a dominant position.

Player

Doubles: spotting your opponents' net position

Despite the many tactical options available to you, sometimes simply looking at your opponents' court position will tell you everything you need to know about what to do.

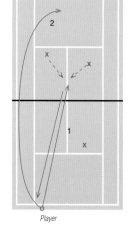

Opponents

➲ **Opponents too far back**
When one or both opponents are positioned a long way from the net, hitting a short, low ball to their feet is a smart option (1). This allows you to move forwards to attack their reply or hit over them (2) once you have forced them to play from a short, low net position.

Player

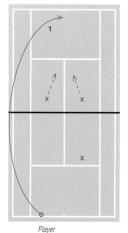

Opponents

Player

➲ **Opponents too close**
When one or both opponents are positioned very close to the net, then the lob becomes your natural first choice of shot (1).

WHAT TO LOOK FOR

Opponents

↻ **Opponents staggered**
↺ **at the net**
Sometimes your opponents will take up a staggered net position (in which one opponent is much closer to the net than the other). In this case, the gap is between them but at an angle – a ball down the middle hit from the side of the court will exploit this (1).

Player

WHAT TO LOOK FOR

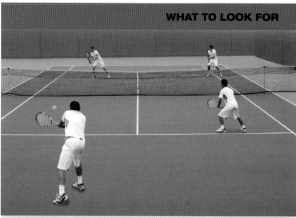

↻ **Opponents too wide**
Playing down the middle of the court may be the best option if you spot your opponents standing too wide of each other at the net.

2 BRINGING OPPONENTS INTO THE NET TO ATTACK

Playing against your opponent at the net can provide a great opportunity to attack, especially if you know he lacks experience or may struggle to volley effectively. Note his volleying technique and court position early on in a match to work out whether this is a viable tactic.

Spotting your opponent's volley weakness

Consider your opponent's grip and swing. An opponent who uses a forehand grip to volley with will be more limited with what he can do with the ball than one who uses a continental grip – and he will find a low volley in particular very difficult to play against. If he also uses a forehand grip for his backhand volley, he will struggle to deal with any sort of pace on the ball.

Your opponent's court position is another good indicator of whether bringing him forwards is a good idea. It is also worth looking at his groundstroke technique.

KEY THINGS TO CONSIDER

▶ **BRING THEM FORWARDS** Look out for the chance to bring opponents into the net since this is a great way to attack also!

▶ **WHERE'S THE SPACE?** Remember that the biggest space on the court when your opponent is at the net is behind them – so using the lob can be more effective than a passing shot when played at the right time.

EXPLOITING YOUR OPPONENT'S GRIP AND SWING — WHAT TO LOOK FOR

∩ **Opponent using forehand grip**
This opponent will struggle with a ball hit with pace because he is using a forehand grip to volley with.

∩ **Opponent using windscreen wiper technique**
A less experienced opponent may not even try to hit a backhand volley. Instead he may use a forehand volley on the other side of his body (the 'windscreen wiper' technique). If this is the case, exposing his backhand side is a must.

∩ **Opponent with big swing**
An opponent who uses a big swing to volley should be challenged with pace (this reduces his preparation time) and balls hit straight at him (cramping the size of his swing).

∩ **Opponent using double-handed grip**
Playing wide of a double-handed volleyer is a smart move because your opponent possesses far less reach than a single-handed player.

⋂ Opponent too far back

If you spot your opponent playing from a very deep court position, bringing him into the net on a ball that you have control over is an option. Remember that hitting the ball short deliberately requires a degree of touch and feel – so choosing the right ball to do this on is crucial. Try not to choose a ball that has put you under too much time, pace or depth pressure.

⋂ Opponent too far to one side

Your opponent may naturally position himself to one side of the baseline to protect a weaker groundstroke. In this case, playing short to the other side will force him to cover maximum distance.

EXPLOITING YOUR OPPONENT'S GROUNDSTROKE TECHNIQUE

WHAT TO LOOK FOR

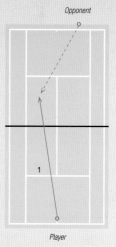

➲ Opponent protecting backhand groundstroke

This right-handed opponent is deliberately protecting his backhand groundstroke. Hit a short ball to his forehand (1) side to force him into covering a lot of court in a short space of time.

↻ Opponent with strong forehand grip

An opponent who uses a strong forehand grip will need to make a big change to play a backhand volley – so bringing him in on his forehand side and then making him hit a backhand volley is a clever tactic (see page 57).

Singles: playing patterns to lure your opponent

Bringing your opponent into the net in order to attack him is a clever tactic that requires excellent shot selection on your part. You need to take into account the effect that your previous shot has had on your opponent, the shot he has played back to you, and where you are both now positioned on the court. Also remember that you don't need to hit a drop shot to bring your opponent forwards – a short ball that stays quite low and is difficult to attack will be sufficient.

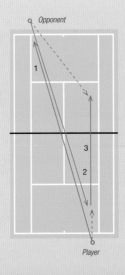

⊂ Crosscourt, then down the line from the advantage court

This player hits a deep crosscourt backhand (1), which pushes his opponent well behind the baseline. The opponent's defensive reply drops quite short (2), allowing the player to move forwards to play a short backhand slice down the line (3). The opponent must now move the maximum distance diagonally in a short space of time.

⊂ Crosscourt, then down the line from the deuce court

The pattern is just as effective from the other side of the court. This time the player hits a deep crosscourt forehand (1) and follows up with a short forehand down the line (3).

◑ Deep crosscourt, then short down the line

One of the most common two-ball patterns to use for this tactic is to play deep crosscourt and then short down the line.

◑ Using a short ball

The player is in total control of this short ball. He plays from inside the baseline with a comfortable contact point around waist height and in front of his body. It is crucial to maintain control over this kind of delicate shot.

WHAT TO DO AFTER A SHORT BALL Your positioning after hitting a short ball (following the two-shot pattern described opposite) depends on how much pressure your opponent is under – similar to when you choose to hit a drop shot (see page 59). Move forwards if you see your opponent under pressure to retrieve the ball because his reply is likely to be short and possibly weak. This may allow you to hit a passing shot from well inside the baseline, or even a volley or smash if you have moved in even closer. Moving forwards also reduces the space available for your opponent to hit into. Note that hitting a lob from this position may not be your best option – especially if you are positioned well inside the baseline because there is less space to hit into from here.

⋂ Move forwards for the volley
If you move in close enough to the net, you could manage a volley or even a smash in this situation.

⋂ Move back to respond
If you sense that your opponent will be able to hit deep once at the net, you need to move back. Moving your position deeper gives you more time to read his shot and decide what your response should be.

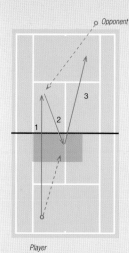

↻ Short backhand, then move forwards
The player moves forwards after hitting a short backhand down the line (1) in anticipation of a short reply (2). He is then able to hit his opponent's defensive shot as a volley winner into the open court (3).

Player

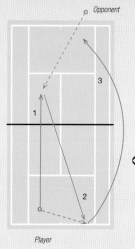

↻ Move back, then lob
This player moves further back as his opponent approaches the net. He then hits a lob over his opponent (3) since this is where the biggest space lies.

Player

Doubles: playing patterns to attack from the back

Deliberately bringing opponents into the net applies just as much in doubles as it does in singles. Again, the most common pattern is to hit deep crosscourt and then short crosscourt, as long as you are in control of the shot. The difference lies in what you do once your opponent is at the net, and here you have a number of possible options.

⋔ Partner intercepts with volley

If your short ball stays low enough, the incoming opponent will have to hit high over the net. This may give your partner at the net a chance to intercept the ball.

➲ Volley between opponents

Hit a short backhand crosscourt (1), which forces your opponent into approaching the net with a high reply (2). This allows your partner at the net to intercept with a winning volley hit between the two opponents (3).

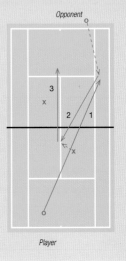

USING THE PASSING SHOT OR LOB A possible alternative to the sneak volley (see right) is to maintain your baseline position and hit either an aggressive passing shot or lob – depending on your opponents' net position. If you see one or both opponents very close to the net, a lob is a great option. If there is a big gap between them, hitting down the middle with pace is a good choice – or consider hitting down the line if one opponent is covering the middle too much.

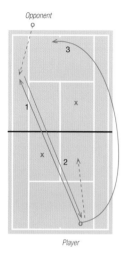

Opponent

Player

♺ **Aggressive lob**
♻ The player brings his opponent into the net (1) and then hits an aggressive lob back over the same opponent's head (3). Once this ball passes the opponent, the player instinctively moves forwards to join his partner at the net. This ability to take the net away from an opposing team is priceless.

USING THE SNEAK VOLLEY If your opponent's approach is hit high but too far wide of your net partner, you could use the sneak volley as an aggressive option. This would mean moving forwards in anticipation of a high, slow reply that you could volley or drive volley through your opponents at the net. This will result in all four players being positioned at the net.

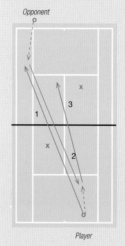

Opponent

Player

♺ **Sneak volley, then**
♻ **move forwards**
Use the sneak volley tactic from the forehand side after hitting a short ball to bring your opponent forwards (1). Hit your opponent's defensive reply (2) as a drive volley straight back down the middle of the court (3).

♻ **Luring opponent into the net**
This player is hitting a short crosscourt forehand in order to bring his baseline opponent into the net. He may choose to hit a lob as a second shot or sneak into the net himself if he senses his opponent is under pressure.

1 The game of tennis today

As improvements are constantly being made to the game in every area, the way in which tennis is played is also changing. This section highlights the most successful playing styles being used in today's game.

See pages 122–123

common game styles

Every tennis player brings a distinctive signature to the game, but certain methods of play are often used to great effect. This chapter analyzes these common styles to help you shape your own game more accurately and then looks at the key differences between how men and women choose to play. It also shows how to examine your personal game style and work out where you need to take your game next.

2 Different types of player

Learn about the most common game styles, including The Aggressive Baseliner; The All-court Player; The Counter-attacker; The Net-rusher; and The Consistent Baseliner.

See pages 124–133

3 Men's and women's tennis: the differences

Differing physical strengths between men and women means there are crucial differences between the two sexes in the way the game is played. Discover what these variables are and how they may affect your own game.

See pages 134–135

4 Examining your own game style

Find out how to pinpoint your strengths in order to develop a winning game style. This section shows how to identify your technical, tactical, physical and mental characteristics and understand how they relate to your game.

See pages 136–139

1 THE GAME OF TENNIS TODAY

Tennis has become a global sport. It is played on every continent, on every surface and by people of all ages, races and social backgrounds. Professional tournaments take place around the globe virtually every week of the year, watched by millions of people worldwide, and the best players are now seen as superstars.

Improvements in equipment, coaching methods and training facilities mean that today's top players are faster, stronger and tougher than ever before – and they are playing the game differently as a result.

An increase in the physicality of the game has resulted in players playing from all areas of the court and using a wide range of technical, tactical, physical and mental skills in order to compete successfully. The very best players are all-rounders, able to compete and win on every surface and against every type of opponent, while still maintaining a specific, recognizable game style, which they develop through many years of competition and practice.

Building a distinct game style allows players to develop the tactics and patterns that suit them best. It helps them to plan practices more specifically and gives them a sharper focus when competing. Therefore, knowing your own game style is vital, since this will drive everything you do on court. It can help you exploit your strengths and limit your weaknesses, as well as set more realistic goals for your game overall.

Understanding your opponent's style quickly allows you to prepare for a match more effectively with a specific set of tactics. Learning about other game styles may also tempt you into experimenting with new methods of play, which you can potentially add to your artillery.

EXAMPLE 1: THE CONSISTENT BASELINER

WHAT TO LOOK FOR:

FAVOURITE GRIP:
50:50 double-handed backhand

STANCE:
Neutral/slightly closed stance to allow weight transfer and balance through the shot.

COURT POSITION:
Hitting close to the baseline in order to use the pace of her opponent's previous shot.

CONTACT POINT:
Just below waist height and comfortably in front of her body.

BODY POSITION:
Note how low she positions herself in order to hit from underneath the ball. Her head remains still and her eyes are fixed firmly on the ball.

LIKELY SHOT:
The direction of her racket face shows that this shot will be hit crosscourt.

For further information on The Consistent Baseliner, see pages 132–133.

EXAMPLE 2: THE AGGRESSIVE BASELINER

WHAT TO LOOK FOR:

FAVOURITE GRIP:
Semi-western forehand

STANCE:
Open/semi-open to allow upper body to fully rotate into the shot.

COURT POSITION:
Attacking baseline position, allowing for an easy transition into the net.

CONTACT POINT:
Will make contact with the ball just as it drops from its peak and just above waist height.

BODY POSITION:
Note how the left arm across the body keeps his upper body turned – allowing him to rotate his upper body into the shot. Note also how he uses a slight knee bend to create energy from the ground upwards.

LIKELY SHOT:
Expect an aggressive forehand played with speed and spin.

For further information on The Aggressive Baseliner, see pages 124–125.

DIFFERENT TYPES OF PLAYER

Learn about the most common game styles used by today's successful players, the skills required to execute each one, and how you can use this information to build your own game style.

The aggressive baseliner

The most commonly used game style on the professional circuit today, the aggressive baseline game style calls on a player to hit aggressive groundstrokes from a variety of baseline positions – with an ability to attack on both the forehand and backhand sides.

WHAT'S HIS STYLE? This player is strong and fast with technique that allows him to produce power and control. A risk-taker, he is prepared to attack from the baseline, but can also defend using guile and creativity. Very often he will finish his points at the net, having created a winning position from the baseline; therefore, an ability to read an opponent's court position and body shape is vital.

HOW TO SPOT HIM The aggressive baseliner plays at least 80 per cent of his shots from the baseline and often has a favourite shot (either forehand or backhand) that he will use as often as possible. For example, look out for the player who runs around his backhand side to hit a forehand. This indicates that he is happy to attack with his forehand from anywhere on the baseline and will probably stay there unless an obvious approach opportunity arises. Compare this with the all-court player, who is happier hitting a backhand to create variety and/or approach the net.

The aggressive baseliner often uses a semi-western grip on his forehand – enabling him to generate pace and spin, and deal with higher-bouncing oncoming balls.

HOW TO BEAT HIM This player performs best against a consistently hit ball with moderate pace – allowing him to find a rhythm, while using some of the pace of the oncoming ball for his aggressive replies. Throw him off his groove by hitting shots with a variety of spin and pace. Shots that drag him away from his preferred baseline position are effective (such as the short-angle slice), while balls that bounce lower and/or slower make it more difficult for him to attack. Alternatively, approach the net regularly to stop him enjoying baseline rallies, but make sure that your approaches put him under enough pressure since he will enjoy hitting on the run and having a target to aim at.

FAVOURITE TACTICS AND GRIP

TACTICS

Every aggressive baseliner uses strong building shots crosscourt to create an opportunity to attack down the line. He pressurizes his opponent with pace, depth and an ability to switch the direction of the ball easily. Hitting deep crosscourt to the opponent's backhand side and then switching down the line to the forehand is a favourite pattern.

➲ **Build, then attack down the line**
The aggressive baseline player hits a deep crosscourt backhand (1), which forces his opponent into hitting short (2). He then moves forwards to attack down the line with his backhand (3).

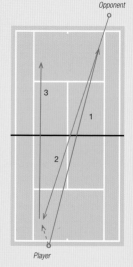

Opponent

Player

KEY GRIP
Semi-western forehand grip

FAMOUS EXAMPLES

Andre Agassi was the ultimate aggressive baseline player. His signature game style was to attack his opponents with punishing groundstrokes from the baseline. Although probably at his best on hard courts, Agassi managed to adjust his style enough to win on all surfaces. He is one of the very few players in history to have won all four Grand Slam Championships.

Serena Williams is considered one of the greatest female players of all time and dominates her opponents with sheer power from the baseline. She uses a number of recognizable patterns of play, which start from a strong serve or return, and she backs up her groundstrokes with solid volleys and smashes at the net. She is an excellent doubles player, too, having won 12 Grand Slam doubles titles to date.

⊃ **Favoured shot: the forehand**
Aggressive baseliners often like to dominate opponents with their forehand.

The all-court player

Recognized as the most creative and versatile player in the game, as he can play a wide range of shots from all areas of the court, the all-court player is often the most exciting to watch. This player is able to fine-tune his tactics depending on his opponent, the court surface and the scoreboard.

WHAT'S HIS STYLE? The all-court player depends on adaptable technique, which allows him to switch between shots smoothly and efficiently. This usually means using grips that are not too extreme (which makes grip changes easier) and using footwork and movement patterns that allow for an easy transition from the baseline to the net. He uses a wider variety of shots than most other players, which means he has more decisions to make. Therefore, his shot selection and general reading of the game need to be first-class.

HOW TO SPOT HIM This player is comfortable playing from all areas of the court. He has strong volley and smash techniques, and often hits with a single-handed backhand as this allows him to play a wider variety of shots and tactics. He also uses the serve-and-volley tactic on occasion, and approaches the net on his return. He is less likely to use extreme grips, so look out for an eastern forehand grip, which allows him to approach the net on shorter, lower balls.

HOW TO BEAT HIM The key to playing against the all-court player is to limit his opportunities to approach the net. This means hitting with enough depth and pace to keep him pinned behind the baseline, so preventing him from moving forwards onto the ball. Hitting the ball high with spin may also cause trouble – particularly against an opponent who uses a single-handed backhand. Make sure you hit a high percentage of first serves in, as this will reduce his chances of approaching the net behind a return.

FAVOURITE TACTICS AND GRIP

TACTICS

The all-court player is an expert at using variety, hitting a wide range of shots that prevent the opponent from finding his own rhythm. Although comfortable playing from the baseline, one of the all-court player's key tactics is to approach the net regularly – especially after playing a short, wide ball that drags his opponent up and off the court.

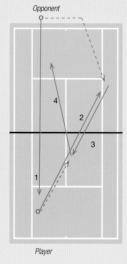

➲ **Short, wide approach**
The all-court player approaches with a short, wide backhand (2). Note how his opponent is forced into moving up the court, allowing the player to move in to volley a reply into the open court (4).

KEY GRIP
Eastern forehand grip

➲ **Strong net play**
An all-court player must be comfortable playing from all areas of the court including the net.

Justine Henin

FAMOUS EXAMPLES

Justine Henin became the world's number-one player by using an all-court game that was simply unique. Her single-handed backhand, once described by John McEnroe as the "greatest backhand in the world", allowed her to mix topspin with slice, baseline with net play and aggression with consistency.

Roger Federer is arguably the greatest player that has ever played the game. He possesses the ultimate all-court game style. His effortless technique, movement and positioning allows him to win from everywhere on the court; his variety and disguise constantly challenge his opponents; and his tactical intelligence means he can make smart decisions in every contest.

The counter-attacker

As a method of play the counter-attacker's game style is becoming more common as the speed of the game continues to increase. This player is more selective as to when he attacks and comfortable dealing with an aggressive opponent, often 'recycling' his opponent's power into an attacking opportunity.

WHAT'S HIS STYLE? The counter-attacker needs speed and agility around the court, with a technique that can handle the pace of a fast oncoming ball. His reaction speed and decision-making need to be sharp because he often has only a split-second to react and deliver a positive response.

The counter-attacker often lures his opponent into attacking to a favoured side or court area. Typically, he leaves a bigger-than-usual space on the court for his opponent to hit into – allowing him to hit aggressively on the run.

HOW TO SPOT HIM The counter-attacker will let you attack him, so look out for a player who doesn't approach the net off relatively short balls or generate a lot of power with his groundstrokes. Often fast and agile around the court, he will spring to life when you approach the net – so make sure you are in command of the point before doing so.

HOW TO BEAT HIM The counter-attacker will want you to hit with pace, so slowing your shots down forces him into creating his own pace instead. If you still want to attack from the baseline, try hitting down the middle more often since this won't give him as much angle to use when countering your aggression. Also, try not to give him an obvious target to aim for – particularly at the net. This means approaching the net selectively – making sure he is under enough pressure so that he can't attack past or over you.

FAVOURITE TACTICS AND GRIP

TACTICS
The counter-attacker often deliberately leaves a space on the baseline for you to hit into – allowing him a chance to race across and attack back at you.

➲ **Leave a gap and set a trap**
Note here how the counter-attacker hits a crosscourt backhand (1) and yet maintains a left-of-centre recovery position. This tempts the opponent into hitting down the line (2) into the bigger space. The counter-attacker can then move across to hit his favourite forehand on the run crosscourt (3) and win the point.

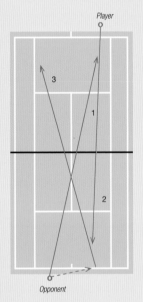

Player

Opponent

KEY GRIP
50:50 double-handed grip

↻ **Recycling the pace**
Counter-attackers typically use the pace of an opponent's ball to attack with themselves.

FAMOUS EXAMPLES

Andy Murray is a master of the counter-attacking game style. He deliberately takes pace off the ball and often lures his opponents into the net to attack past or over them. He mixes aggression with consistency and accuracy, and has the most incredible defensive capabilities. He also has the ability to step up the court and dominate with strong serves and groundstrokes when necessary.

Martina Hingis won five Grand Slam singles titles by playing with great efficiency from the baseline. Her simple and effortless technique allowed her to absorb the pace of the ball and counter with precision and intelligence.

The net-rusher

Moving forwards as often as possible, the net-rusher's aim is to dominate his opponent at the net. This player typically uses a combination of strong serves and groundstrokes to approach with, and covers the net with solid volleys and smashes. He enjoys playing short points and putting his opponents under immediate pressure in the rally. The net-rusher is a risk-taker who must be able to handle the emotional rollercoaster that this style brings.

WHAT'S HIS STYLE? This style of play is less common today as many players are comfortable playing against an opponent at the net. Improvements in players' physical speed and strength allow them to hit passing shots and lobs from all areas of the court – with many players enjoying a target at the net to aim at. However, players who predominantly use other styles of play still use the net-rusher's tactics as a great way of mixing up their own game.

HOW TO SPOT HIM The net-rusher's style suits players with big serves who like to attack straight away. This often includes tall players who can cover large court areas at the net. When warming up at the start of a match, this player wastes no time in coming forwards to practise volleys and smashes – this should give you a great clue.

The net-rusher often uses a single-handed backhand as it allows him to hit with slice, offering him an effective way of approaching the net. Therefore, look out for players using a single-handed eastern backhand grip.

⌒ Finishing at the net
Being able to finish points at the net is a crucial part of the net-rusher's game.

HOW TO BEAT HIM A net-rusher want to pressurize you into hitting winners past him as soon as he approaches the net, but remember that you don't have to win the point straight away – even if he has moved forwards. Try to use the two-ball pass tactic (see pages 106–109) as often as possible. This means making the net-rusher play his first volley by hitting straight at him, with a view to hitting a winning pass or lob on your second attempt. Quite often, a more natural space will open up for you once you've made your opponent play his first volley.

Also, when in a baseline rally, maintain a good length to your shots – making it more difficult for your opponent to approach the net from this deep position. Finally, taking the net away from a net-rusher will frustrate him more than anything else, so look for your own opportunities to approach before he does.

FAVOURITE TACTICS AND GRIP

TACTICS
The net-rusher's two signature tactics are the serve and volley and the chip and charge. Both involve approaching the net as soon as the rally begins and aim to put immediate pressure on the opponent.

⇨ Down the line approach
The net-rusher uses his second serve return as a way of approaching – slicing his backhand down the line and closing in on the net quickly (2). Note how he follows the line of the ball and then covers the line and middle of the court most of all – forcing the opponent into trying to hit a difficult crosscourt passing shot (3).

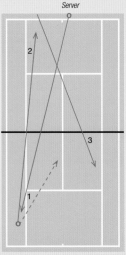

Server

Returner

KEY GRIP
Eastern backhand grip

FAMOUS EXAMPLES

Pete Sampras became one of the most successful players of all time by using a serve-and-volley tactic that continued to pressurize his opponents — particularly on the grass courts of Wimbledon, where he won seven times.

Martina Navratilova won a total of 59 Grand Slam titles (singles, doubles and mixed doubles) and much of her success was down to her ability to dominate from the net. When serving she would often use the serve-and-volley tactic combined with the chip-and-charge return. Her physical prowess and outstanding net skills made her arguably the best female player ever to play the game.

The consistent baseliner

The game style of the consistent baseliner requires a player to hit consistently accurate groundstrokes from the baseline and go for long stretches in a match without making any unforced errors. This requires great concentration and poise, and an ability to dig deep in longer rallies.

WHAT'S HIS STYLE? The consistent baseliner's style of play is becoming less common in today's professional game simply because the physicality of tennis has increased so much. There are far fewer neutral moments in a baseline rally, in which both players are only hitting for consistency. Players now look to hit aggressively from the baseline with the intention of building an attacking position. In other words, almost every groundstroke is viewed as an opportunity to attack.

However, consistency, accuracy and patience remain great qualities for a tennis player – particularly for juniors keen to develop their game. At an amateur level, the vast majority of points are won through an opponent's error – forced or unforced – so maintaining a solid back court game will provide a great foundation for success.

HOW TO SPOT HIM This player takes far fewer risks than the majority of players and is content to stay on the baseline even when the oncoming ball drops short. He usually plays very consistently on both sides, but won't necessarily possess a big forehand or backhand. He relies on his opponents' errors to win most of his points, so will have stamina and be able to concentrate for long periods of time. He often uses a more extreme grip on his forehand side because there is less of a need to transition between the baseline and the net. Look out for a player using a western forehand grip; this suits the consistent baseline game style most of all.

⌒ Baseline strength
Consistency from the baseline provides the foundation for this player's tactics.

HOW TO BEAT HIM It is difficult to outlast a consistent baseliner, so changing the feel of the point is a smart move. This may mean approaching the net yourself – forcing him into hitting past or over you immediately. Another option is to bring him forwards deliberately, so forcing him into hitting volleys and smashes that he may not feel comfortable with. Alternatively, try rallying from the baseline but mixing up the pace, preventing him from playing with any rhythm.

FAVOURITE TACTICS AND GRIP

TACTICS
The consistent baseliner relies on his opponent's errors, so doesn't try to dominate the point with a specific pattern of play. However, be prepared for him to hit consistently and accurately for long periods of the match. He often trades crosscourt, choosing the lowest part of the net and longest part of the court to hit into. He also defends high and deep crosscourt, and makes his opponent play as many volleys and smashes as possible if faced with an opponent at the net.

⊃ Trading crosscourt
This diagram shows the target area into which the consistent baseliner will want to hit the majority of his groundstrokes.

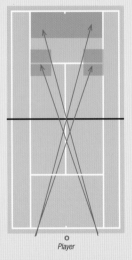

Player

KEY GRIP
Western forehand grip

FAMOUS EXAMPLES

Michael Chang was one of the most consistent baseline players of all time. He combined speed and stamina with fierce concentration and focus, and was rewarded by winning the French Open singles title in 1989 – becoming the youngest Grand Slam winner of all time. This record still stands today.

Chris Evert, a former world number one, dominated women's tennis with the strength of her baseline game. Her forehand and backhand were hit with great timing and precision, and her tactical intelligence was unrivalled.

MEN'S AND WOMEN'S TENNIS:
THE DIFFERENCES

Today, there is a considerable difference in the way tennis is played by the best male and female players in the world. Significant physical discrepancies have meant that female players are using different techniques and playing from different court positions compared with their male counterparts.

COURT POSITION Female players often prefer to play closer to the baseline, using simple, efficient techniques to recycle the pace of the oncoming ball (in order to hit with power themselves) and using shorter swings that are easy to coordinate. In contrast, male players tend to play from deeper court positions as this enables them to generate more power themselves. This leads to longer and more complex swing techniques with the use of more parts of the body in their shots.

BALL CHARACTERISTICS The different court positions favoured by men and women has led to different tactics being used. Because of their closer baseline position, female players hit the ball with a flatter trajectory and less spin – using a narrower range of angles to attack with as a result. With their deeper court position, male players have more of the court and its surroundings to hit into – which means they can play with a wider variety of trajectories, spins and angles. This leads to more varied tactics and game styles being used on the men's tour.

SERVING AND RETURNING Male players often rely more heavily on their serve, while the key shot in women's tennis now is the return of serve. Both sexes build specific patterns of play and signature strengths around these two vital playing situations. In general, male players try to dominate more often with their forehand groundstroke after serving, while female players choose to attack with a more equal ratio of forehands to backhands from the back court.

NET PLAY When it comes to playing from the net, male players often take more risks and approach more frequently, whereas female players are more selective about when they play from the front of the court. Women will often build a commanding position from the baseline first before finishing the point from the net. As a result, research shows that women are more effective at the net than men – highlighting the fact that they are more selective in their approaches.

RALLY LENGTH We are also seeing a difference in the length of rallies in men's and women's tennis. Female players are adopting more of a 'first strike' mentality (looking to attack at the first available opportunity) with the length of their rallies becoming shorter as a result. The key tactic in women's tennis is to hit as often and aggressively as possible away from the opponent. The opposite is true in men's tennis where, due to the high-quality defensive skills of today's players, rallies are lasting longer because it is becoming harder to put the ball away.

SO, WHAT OF THE FUTURE FOR TENNIS? The differences in style between the sexes are not necessarily the ones we will see in the future. It's likely that the female game will gravitate more towards the male game as players continue to adapt and develop their athletic abilities. Playing from the net may also become more important, as players seek to counter the current dominance of aggressive baseliners, while all-court players, with their ability to play a range of different game styles, may conquer all.

↻ **Rafael Nadal**
Rafael Nadal hits with a huge amount of topspin on his groundstrokes, which makes the ball kick high, deep and often wide of the court.

4 EXAMINING YOUR OWN GAME STYLE

Every successful player uses a personal game style – a blend of the technical, tactical, physical and mental skills that form a distinct playing identity. This style is shaped over many years through match play and practice, and constantly evolves throughout a player's career. Building a distinct game style allows you to develop tactics and playing patterns that suit you best. It helps you plan practices more specifically and gives you sharper focus when competing. Therefore, knowing your own game is vital because it will drive everything you do on the court.

Technical and tactical factors

It is impossible to separate technique from tactics since the way you hit the ball will influence how you play the game, but the way in which you play can also affect how you hit the ball. So, make sure that your techniques complement the way you are trying to play the game. Quite often, a player's technique won't fit his tactics, and this can result in disappointing performances and results. As an example, imagine a

player with an extreme forehand grip who wants to play at the net as often as possible. The big grip change necessary between his forehand groundstroke and his volley will make this very difficult. Therefore, he either needs to adjust his forehand grip (to make the transition smoother) or play more from the baseline and wait for a slower, higher ball that gives him more time to switch grips.

DO YOU USE A MILDER GRIP? In general, players who use milder grips – continental and eastern forehands, eastern single-handed backhands and 50:50 double-handed backhands – for their groundstrokes can make the transition to the net more easily. They require smaller grip changes and often hit with neutral stances (front foot directly in front of back foot), allowing their body momentum to carry them forwards naturally. They are comfortable moving forwards against lower-bouncing balls hit at around waist height – a perfect match for their technique.

Using a milder grip also means these players can hit a wider variety of shots in a rally as they can change grips smoothly and quickly. For instance, an all-court player using an eastern forehand can move to hit a backhand slice, backhand drive, drop shot, volley and smash quite easily. This is why the all-court player and the net-rusher (see pages 126–127 and 130–131) lean towards playing with these techniques.

DO YOU USE A MORE EXTREME GRIP? Players who use more extreme grips – semi-western and western forehands, strong eastern single-handed and 75:25 double-handed backhands – will favour baseline play because these grips help create more spin and can be played more effectively against a higher-bouncing ball. However, it isn't as easy to switch these grips to a volley and smash grip, meaning that players need to approach and play from the net more selectively. The aggressive baseliner and consistent baseline players (see pages 124–125 and 132–133) are well suited to this way of playing.

So, think about the way you hit the ball – does it match the way you want to play? Consider the grips you use – do they allow you to play from the court area you prefer? Think also about when you play your best tennis – where and how do you win your points?

➲ Perfect playing technique
This player's technique is a perfect match for his aggressive baseline game style.

Physical factors

Different game styles in tennis call for slightly different physical skills. The aggressive baseline player, for example, needs speed and strength. The consistent baseliner requires a good dose of stamina, while the net-rusher must have agility and balance in order to cover the net efficiently and effectively.

The way a player is built also has a huge influence on what is possible. Often, the small, agile player will play more from the baseline, happy to stay in the rally and wait for an opportunity to attack or to sneak in to the net to finish the point. This player may struggle to generate pace himself, so will often play close to the baseline and use the speed of the oncoming ball for his next shot. These physical traits naturally suit the game style of the counter-attacker and consistent baseliner (see pages 128–129 and 132–133).

Taller players who are lean and flexible tend to play more from the net – with the ability to cover the ground between the baseline and net swiftly, as well as cover the space at the net with their longer reach. These players will often serve and volley and use the return as an approach shot when possible. These physical traits suit the all-court and net-rusher game styles (see pages 126–127 and 130–131).

So, do your physical strengths suit the way you want to play the game? Does the way you are built match your game style?

⊃ Perfect baseline timing
This player uses excellent timing from the baseline to recycle the pace of her opponent's shot to her advantage.

⋂ Physical prowess
This player's speed and strength help him transition effectively from the baseline to the net.

⋂ Adopt a good ready position
Make sure you start in a good ready position in order to maximize your physical strengths every time you play.

◑ Doubles: communication is key
In doubles, communicating well with your partner can help you maintain both your focus and positive energy.

◑ Develop good mental strength
It is crucial to fully commit to your shots both mentally and physically, whatever your style of play.

➲ Work with a professional
Working with a coach will help you to build a genuine understanding of your game.

Psychological factors

Your attitude on the court will also have an influence on how you play the game. Therefore, just as with all the other performance factors, it's crucial to match your mental skills to your game style. For example, to play an aggressive game, you need a robust attitude – one that can handle the emotion of winning and losing points quickly. You need to be able to take risks and accept the consequences, while maintaining an ability to think straight and make smart decisions. The aggressive baseliner and the net-rusher need this most of all.

The all-court player will find that he has an array of tactical options available to him – more than any other style of player. He can choose to stay back, move forwards or even bring his opponent forwards, and will have a wide variety of shots to choose from. Therefore, if you want to play this style of game you need to bring enough tactical intelligence to the court to allow you to narrow down your options quickly and easily.

The consistent baseliner and the counter-attacker need to have stubborn streaks and the determination not to give up on any ball. They need to be able to concentrate for long periods without necessarily taking as many risks as other types of player. To play this way you require tenacity and the ability to accept that your opponent is going to want to attack you – sometimes successfully!

So, think about your mental strengths – what style of play are they suited to? Are you a risk-taker? Do you enjoy having choices to make or do you prefer to keep things simple? Do you enjoy being the aggressor or the defender?

Learning more about your game

You can analyze your game using profiling, testing, goal setting, match charting, coaching and videoing. These tools will help you understand your strengths and weaknesses both physically and psychologically. For example, video analysis gives you feedback on how you hit the ball and if your technique is aligned with how you want to play. You can also discover more about your physical strengths and weaknesses by taking part in a tennis-specific physical test – covering areas such as speed, agility, strength, endurance and flexibility – which will highlight the areas you are strong in and the ones needing more work! Filling in a technical and tactical profile sheet (see opposite page) can also raise your awareness of how you play best and give you a starting point for setting yourself specific goals to achieve within your game.

TECHNICAL AND TACTICAL PROFILE SHEET

MY GAME STYLE
1: Aggressive baseliner
2:
3:

ROLE MODEL(S)
1: Novak Djokovic
2: Andy Murray
3:

MAIN STRENGTHS
1: Powerful forehand and consistent backhand
2: Speed around the court
3: Never-say-die attitude

KEY AREAS TO WORK ON
1: Serving accuracy and consistency - straighter ball toss
2: Volley technique - keep wrist firmer on contact
3: Choosing when to approach net - recognize opportunities quicker

" PLAY MY BEST TENNIS WHEN I..."
1: Warm up thoroughly before a match
2: Start the match by not making many unforced errors
3: Keep my mind in the present and don't think about the outcome of the match

KEY DRILLS TO USE
1: x 20 serving target practice before a match
2: Crosscourt then switch down the line drill
3: Alternating deep and short ball drill

PHYSICAL SKILLS REQUIRED
1: Speed and endurance
2: Shoulder flexibility and suppleness
3: Leg strength as my serve develops

MENTAL SKILLS REQUIRED
1: Strong emotional control when the score is close
2: Maintain tenacity and determination even when losing
3: Ability to read my opponent's game early in the match

COMPETITION GOALS
1: Win my singles league
2: Gain selection for club doubles team
3: Improve ranking to next level

OTHER COMMENTS
1: Need to commit to more regular coaching sessions
2: Enter more tournaments in the summer season
3:

GLOSSARY

Advantage court The left-hand side of the court from which the server serves to (i.e. left of the centre mark).

Aggressive baseliner A player who uses aggressive groundstrokes from the baseline to win the majority of his points.

Aggressive loop A groundstroke that is hit high over the net with topspin, played with the intention of pushing the opponent deep (and often wide).

All-court player A player who is comfortable playing from all areas of the court and who is capable of finishing points at the net.

Anticipation The ability to predict the most likely outcome of the opponent's next shot.

Approach shot A shot hit with the deliberate intention of coming in to the net after it is hit.

Attacking shot A shot that creates an opportunity to finish the point.

Back behind A wrong-footing shot that is hit back in the direction of an opponent's previous shot. It is most effectively played when an opponent anticipates a shot to the other side of the court.

Backswing The way a player takes his racket back before swinging forwards to hit the ball.

Ball characteristics The varying ways the ball flies through the air after being hit – namely height, direction, depth, speed and spin.

Ball toss The way a player throws the ball in the air in order to hit a serve.

Ball trajectory The type of movement (the shape) the ball takes as it flies through the air.

Baseline The line at either end of the court (parallel to the net) from which the server serves.

Baseline player A player who relies on strong groundstrokes hit from the baseline to win the majority of his points.

Baseline rally A point that is played with both of the players hitting groundstrokes from a baseline position.

Block A short, 'punched' groundstroke that is usually hit for control against a fast oncoming ball. It is often used as a return against a strong serve.

Body serve A serve that is deliberately hit in the direction of the returner's body to 'cramp' the returner's swing.

Both back A doubles formation that sees both players in the same pair positioned at the baseline.

Building shot A shot that puts a player in an advantageous position in the rally.

Chip and charge A tactic used when a player hits his sliced return of serve as an approach shot. It is a planned approach tactic that is often used against a second serve.

Closed stance A shot that is hit with a player's front foot positioned in front of and across their back foot.

Consistent baseliner A player who wins the majority of his points by hitting consistent groundstrokes from the baseline.

Contact point The point of impact between the oncoming ball and the player's racket.

Counter-attacker A player who absorbs the pace of his opponent's shot and sends the ball back with a high degree of accuracy and consistency. A counter-attacker generally prefers the opponent to attack first in the rally.

Court position The position on the court that a player, or team of players, takes up.

Crosscourt shot A shot played diagonally across the court from either the right or left side.

Defending shot A shot that attempts to prevent the opponent from finishing the point.

Deuce court The right-hand side of the court from which the server serves (i.e. right of the centre mark).

Diagonal movement When a player moves diagonally across the court to the ball.

Double bluff When a player fakes a movement to one side of the court only to cover the other side instead.

Double-handed A player who keeps both hands on his racket during the shot. This is usually seen on backhand groundstrokes in particular.

Down the line A shot played straight down the court from either the right or left side.

Drive volley A volley hit using groundstroke technique that creates pace and spin on the ball.

Drop shot A shot that is deliberately hit very short over the net. It is usually played best when the opponent is positioned deep behind the baseline.

Finish volley A volley used to finish a point.

Flight path The way the oncoming ball moves through the air.

Floating ball A ball that crosses high over the net without much pace.

Footwork The way a player positions himself for his next shot. This could include movement towards, around or away from the ball.

Forced error When a player forces his opponent into making an error.

Game situation The court position that players play from in tennis. There are five main game situations: serving, returning, both back, net play and opponent's net play.

Game style A player's game style is shaped by his physical, psychological, technical and tactical ability and represents how he plays the game.

Grip How a player holds the racket in order to play. There are a number of different grips that can be used in tennis.

Groundstroke A shot hit after the ball has bounced, either from the forehand or backhand side.

High-percentage shot A shot hit with a high margin of error (e.g. into a big target area).

Inside-out forehand When a player deliberately runs around his backhand side to hit a forehand crosscourt. The inside-out backhand is the opposite.

Instinctive approach When a player decides to approach the net after seeing the effectiveness of his previous shot.

Intercept volley In doubles, when the partner of either the server or returner intercepts a crosscourt rally with a volley.

Junk ball A ball that is hit deliberately to throw an opponent off their rhythm. This could include hitting with no pace, a different type of spin or to an awkward place on the court.

Lateral movement When a player moves sideways across the baseline to the ball.

Lob A shot hit high over the head of an opponent at the net. It can be hit in singles or in doubles as an aggressive or defensive shot.

Margin of error The amount of error a player allows himself for every shot. Some shots will be hit with a higher margin of error than others.

Middle serve A serve hit down the middle of the service box from either the deuce or advantage court.

Mirror return A return of serve that is hit straight back at the server – usually back down the middle of the court.

Net rusher A player who wins the majority of his points at the net with strong volleys and smashes.

Neutral stance A shot hit with a player's front foot positioned directly in front and in line with their back foot so their hips face sideways to the court.

One up/one back A common doubles formation that sees one player positioned at the net and his partner positioned on the baseline.

Open stance A shot hit with a player's front foot positioned alongside his back foot so his hips face forwards.

Parallel play In doubles, when playing partners move forwards, sideways and backwards together to prevent big gaps from opening between them on the court.

Passing shot A groundstroke played when an opponent is approaching or at the net. The passing shot can be played crosscourt, down the line or straight at the net opponent.

Patterns of play The sequence of shots a player uses to execute his favoured tactics.

Perception The ability to read the characteristics of the oncoming ball.

Planned approach When a player decides to approach the net before hitting his shot – no matter what the outcome.

Ready position The position a player takes when his opponent is about to hit the ball.

Receiving skills The ability to read the game by receiving an opponent's shots through good anticipation, perception, preparation and movement.

Recovery The desire to move back to a central court position before the opponent hits their next shot.

Return The shot that a player hits back after his opponent serves to him.

Returning stance The position on the court that a player takes up when he is about to return serve. This may differ for a first serve return compared to a second serve return.

Serve The way a player starts the point. Serves are hit alternately from the deuce and advantage courts.

Serve and volley The tactic of approaching the net with a serve with a view to finishing the point with a winning volley.

Short angle A shot that is hit to a short and wide area of the court. This could be a groundstroke, return, volley or smash.

Shot selection The decision a player takes when choosing what type of shot to hit next.

Slice A type of spin a player puts on the ball when hitting a groundstroke, serve or volley. Slice tends to make the ball 'slide' off the court with a low bounce.

Slice serve A serve that is hit with slice.

Smash A shot that is hit against a ball that travels over and above the head of a player at the net. It is hit using serve technique and requires precise positioning underneath the ball.

Sneak approach A type of approach that sees a player deciding to move forwards to the net after seeing the effectiveness of his shot.

Split-step A small step with both feet (also known as a check step or de-weighting) that balances the body and allows a player to move in any direction as the opponent is about to hit the ball.

Stance The way a player stands on the court as he hits a shot.

Swing shape The way a player swings his racket before, during and after making contact with the ball.

Switch shot A groundstroke that is hit down the line from a crosscourt rally.

Tactical anticipation The ability to predict the most likely shot from an opponent based on his court position and previous playing patterns.

Tactics The method of play a player uses to win his points with.

Technical anticipation The ability to predict the most likely shot from an opponent based on the technique he is about to use.

Time pressure The pressure applied to an opponent by restricting the time he has to hit his next shot.

Topspin A type of spin a player puts on the ball when hitting a groundstroke, serve or volley. Topspin tends to kick higher after the bounce than other shots.

Topspin serve A serve that is hit with topspin. The ball kicks off the ground with a high bounce.

Trading shot A shot that maintains a neutral balance of play in a point. Also referred to as a rallying shot.

Two-ball pass A tactic that requires a player to deliberately hit a high-percentage passing shot with the aim of making an opponent play a volley – with the intention of hitting a winning pass or lob with his second shot.

Variety of shot The ability to hit a range of different shots in a match.

Volley A shot that is hit before the ball is allowed to bounce.

Wide serve A serve hit to the wide corner of the service box from either the deuce or advantage court.

Winner A shot that an opponent cannot reach (or barely touches with his racket).

INDEX

Publisher's Acknowledgements
Marshall Editions would like to thank the following agencies for supplying images for inclusion in this book:

page 1 David Lee/Shutterstock; pages 2–3 David Madison/Getty Images; page 4 Sportlibrary/Shutterstock; page 5 Joe Belanger/Shutterstock; page 7 Olga Besnard/Shutterstock; pages 8–9 AFP/Getty Images; pages 10–11 Neale Cousland/Shutterstock; pages 12, 14, 18 Sportlibrary/Shutterstock; pages 20–21 Sportlibrary/Shutterstock; pages 22, 32, 34 fstockfoto/Shutterstock; pages 46–47 bikeriderlondon/Shutterstock; pages 48, 54, 57, 60 JosePaulo/Shutterstock; pages 68–69 sportgraphic/Shutterstock; pages 70, 80, 86 Paul Maguire/Shutterstock; pages 88–89 Stockbyte/Getty Images; pages 90, 96, 102 sportgraphic/Shutterstock; pages 104–105 Jose Gil/Shutterstock; pages 106, 114 Neale Cousland/Shutterstock; pages 120–121 Neale Cousland/Shutterstock; pages 122, 124, 134, 136 Foodpics/Shutterstock; page 125 top Anthony Correia/Shutterstock; page 127 Galina Barskaya/Shutterstock; page 129 Neale Cousland/Shutterstock; page 131 Clive Brunskill/Getty Images; page 133 Sports Illustrated/Getty Images; page 134 Neale Cousland/Shutterstock; page 135 Getty Images; pages 140–141, 142–143 Paul Maguire/Shutterstock; page 144 JosePaulo/Shutterstock

All other images are the copyright of Marshall Editions. While every effort has been made to credit contributors, Marshall Editions would like to apologize should there have been any omissions or errors and would be pleased to make the appropriate correction to future editions of the book.

Author's Acknowledgements
A big thank you to Sorrel Wood and Philippa Davis at Marshall Editions for helping turn this book into a reality, and to Caroline West and Mark Latter at Blue Dragonfly Limited for their expert project-management, editorial and design skills. Thanks also to Simon Ainley and Dan Thorp for their invaluable tennis knowledge and to Simon Pask for his outstanding photography.

Special thanks go to the Lawn Tennis Association for the use of their National Tennis Centre, in London, where the special photography took place. Finally, thanks to Dan Betts, Hannah Collin, Rob Fullagar, Anna Hawkins, Gabrielle Paul, Charlotte Pearce, Miguel Santana, and Niall Stewart for doing a great job of modeling such an array of tennis shots and situations.

Dedication
To my wonderful wife Catherine and our three fantastic boys Jake, Scott and Luke.